ALTURA EXTREMA

ALTIPLANO

ESCALERA

AMAZONÍA

CHAZUTA

C
E
N
T
R
A
L

CENTRAL

Virgilio Martínez

WITH
NICHOLAS GILL

PHOTOGRAPHS BY
JIMENA AGOIS &
ERNESTO BENAVIDES

8 • 23

29 • 39

40 • 53

54 • 79

80 • 93

94 • 119

120 • 137

INTRODUCTION

MARCONA

MANGLARALAR

ORILLA

BAJO ANDINO

ANDE

ALTURA EXTREMA

138 • 159	160 • 185	186 • 211	212 • 233	234 • 241	242 • 249	250 • 253

ALTIPLANO   ESCALERA   AMAZONÍA   CHAZUTA   CRYSTALES   GLOSSARY   INDEX

Somewhere outside of Marcona, a small fishing village on the coast south of Ica, out in the sea, a few meters below the surface, on the ocean floor, there's a rock. On that rock are limpets, small gastropods that eat the sargassum, and a brown macro algae, which also lives on the rock. There are crabs on the rock. They eat the limpets. The survival of each species depends upon the other. There is a reason why they are all here.

In Lamay, high in the Andes near Urubamba, a subsistence farmer has a thriving garden full of beautiful, shiny tree tomatoes. Beside it there is *kiwicha* and beneath the ground are beets. Sometimes they rotate the crops and plant *tarwi*, which puts back into the soil what the other plants took away. With no scientific support or technical understanding, their wisdom and agricultural knowledge comes from a strong heritage and deep connection to the earth and surroundings.

In a dry forest outside of Piura, in the far north of Peru, there's an avocado grove where the avocados are big and round. You can pick them and eat them like apples. Surrounding them are fences made of rows of two other trees, cactus and *algarrobo*, which are some of the very few other plants that can thrive in this arid place where rain is a rarity. I'm not entirely sure what the relationship between the plants is here, but I know that there is a reason they are found together. That's why, as I have done with the other examples above, put them on a plate together.

At Central we cook ecosystems. The plate has to communicate what we experience in nature. When we think about the ingredients that make up a dish, we are thinking about the entire dish. Not a single ingredient is prized more than another. Each is as integral to the recipe as it is to its own ecosystem.

When we discover these groups of ingredients together and bring them back into the kitchen to find a way that allows them to harmonize on the plate, far from their own environment, it doesn't always happen instantly. Sometimes there are easier ways. Shortcuts. We could swap one ingredient for another—something from outside their realm of origin, and the entire dish would taste better. Yet respecting this harmony is stronger than the flavors, though we have found more often than not, over time and practice as we search for greater balance, nothing needs to be forced. It happens naturally.

Today, in Peru, informal gold miners dump mercury in the Amazonian rivers, oil and logging companies are clearing huge swaths of rainforest, warming global temperatures are melting glaciers, and increasingly drastic wet and dry seasons have left high altitude potato farmers without water and the natural world on the brink of collapse. Consequently, there is no more significant moment to think about the balance and harmony of Peru's flora and fauna that have managed to survive and evolve amongst each other.

To make this concept fully realized, we chose to lose many of the basic things we've become accustomed to in the kitchen. We've chosen to renounce all products and textures not found naturally in Peru—common things that have become standard cooking tools among restaurants worldwide, like fancy powders, industrial sweeteners, magic thickeners, and untraceable oils—and replace them entirely with ingredients found within our environment in Peru. Our proudest achievement at Central, it has been a long, gradual process that has repeatedly challenged and pushed us in new directions we never thought were possible.

In time, we realized that we already have everything we need. In Puno, on the vast, treeless plateau that is the *altiplano*, quinoa powder is used as a thickener in soups. In Puerto Maldonado, in the jungle, macerated fruits are used to sweeten. It dawned on us: If we are so rich with resources, why do we have to import unnecessary ingredients from elsewhere? Instead of importing flour, we should be creating some sort of substitution from what we have here.

To do this—using only ingredients native to Peru—we had to change our entire way of thinking, as well as logistics. We created a system of Peruvian ingredients that we could use to replace these untraceable products that not just our kitchen, but every kitchen in the world has become accustomed to. We discovered we could use ancient ingredients like *tocosh*, a form of fermented potato from the high Andes, as thickeners. A high-jungle cactus called *airampo* and cochineal insects could be used as colorants. "Why can't we just use xanthan gum?" someone in the kitchen would ask. "It would be so much easier." Yes, indeed it would be. Instead, we use *chuño de mashua*, a freeze-dried root from the *altiplano*, fueled with our identity.

Usually in cooking you have exact measurements and methods, but because this is so new, we're still experimenting with what thickeners, sweeteners, and dyes we use, how they are used, and how we make them. We are in a constant state of evolution. We have to test everything in the different ways it can be used and at what temperatures. We might go back and forth in a recipe, using *chuño* to thicken or *pacae* crystals to sweeten, trying to strike the right balance. Sometimes something like a high amount of fat in a fish or piece of meat can throw off the equation we thought we had right.

Or sometimes we accidently add too much gel made of *huampo* and that mistake actually makes it better. We're always searching for the right ingredient that gives us the flexibility in the way we want. This method of trial and error makes things harder, but we feel it's worth it. We have found that our food is more pure than it was when we used industrial products that made things so much easier.

The early transition into this concept was confusing for us. It was difficult to trace the origin of many of the ingredients and, in turn, connect with all of the people involved in producing them. After several years with little notice, the media was suddenly coming in and talking to us and we were distracted. It all happened quickly and we weren't always prepared for the attention. It would have been easy just to surrender to what was expected in terms of flavors and colors, to be like the other kitchens and use imported products, but ultimately, we had to be true to ourselves; it was more important to us than pleasing everyone.

I started skateboarding around eleven years old and fell in love with it. It quickly became my life and helped give me a sense of creativity. When you're skateboarding, you are always performing; you need to be imaginative to find spots to skate; you have to work hard and commit; you have to work in teams with different types of people. It's very mentally and physically grueling. Looking back, I can see the foundation of how I work and interact with people in the kitchen now forming then. Curiously enough, the adults saw us as lazy, rebellious kids, but actually, we were very driven. Everyone I skated with has gone on to do something successful, and is probably enjoying it as much as skateboarding. It was a good school for all of us.

Growing up in Peru, being a professional skateboarder wasn't much of a reality. For one, it was expensive. I broke boards all of the time and the soles of my shoes wore down quickly. At seventeen, I went to a skate park in California where sponsors and managers were looking for young talent—this was my chance for a career. I was in the middle of a 360 spin on a half pipe and in an instant I lost control. I was suddenly falling through the air in a free fall, my entire future hanging in the balance. I landed on my shoulder, breaking it, and the doctor told me I needed immediate surgery. But because I didn't have insurance, I had to fly back to Peru, my body pumped full of chemicals. Two weeks after that shoulder healed, I broke the other one. After about eight years of skating, two bad shoulders, and no sponsors, it was time to rethink my options.

My family was never truly supportive of my skating career. My father and brother, both lawyers, are much more traditional and wanted me to follow in their footsteps. I thought it was time to do something safe and enrolled in law school. I liked reading and studying, but something was missing. It was hard for me to stay in one place. Law meant a future of sitting in an office and I didn't feel I would have the sense of freedom I really wanted.

When I was younger, whenever I could, I used to surf in San Bartolo, a beach town south of Lima. On my board I was surrounded by fish and fishermen, this life of the sea. I would paddle my board up to a boat where the fishermen were eating ceviche with the fish they had just caught. Those were the first ceviches I'd ever tried. I'd hang out with the fishermen and chat about life. In small shacks on the shore I would have *arroz con mariscos*, or be shucking oysters, sea urchins, and clams, and eat them raw. These were the good days that were always in the back of my mind: I appreciated food and seeing where it came from, but even more than that, I appreciated the freedom I had then. Cooking in Peru then was not like it is now. There were no famous chefs or culinary figures to look up to. I wasn't even particularly passionate about cooking. I just wanted to get away. In those days, everyone my age dreamed of leaving. I read gastronomy books all of the time and I wanted to learn more things and get to know the world. I had to find something I was compelled to do. Studying law prevented that, so I dropped out. With no options in Lima, I enrolled in culinary school in Ottawa, Canada.

Ottawa was new to me, so it felt good to be there. It was clean and secure, much different than Lima during that time. Cooking still wasn't my primary passion and after a year I was restless again; I wanted to go somewhere more exciting—a bigger city. I transferred to another culinary school, this time in London, which, for a nineteen-year-old, was a great place to live. It was there that I entered a real restaurant kitchen for the first time. I worked at the Ritz Hotel, which had a very classic structure with a focus on French cuisine. My eyes began to open to the possibilities of what cooking could accomplish, but after a year and a half my visa was up and, while I wanted to stay, I couldn't get an extension.

With a one-way ticket back to Lima in my hand, I was disappointed. I felt that I hadn't accomplished everything I set out to do. I had a layover in New York and when I landed, I didn't get on the next flight. I just couldn't. I wanted to experience New York.

After asking around to see what restaurant work was available, I found myself at Lutèce, one of the best restaurants in the city at the time. As I began to immerse myself in the basics, I started to take my job very seriously.

Lutèce was a fun restaurant. The French, who had cooked in many of the world's great kitchens, were on the top floor. Down below were all the Latinos— the Mexicans and the Ecuadorians— who had harrowing stories of crossing the border. I became the go-between for the two groups. I felt like the kitchen was my place. These were all my people. I worked hard to stay organized and to understand the balance of flavors; I made countless lobster risottos, tuna mille-feuilles, and consommés; I worked with precious ingredients I was not used to, like cheeses and wines from France, the best black truffles from the Dordogne, tuna from Japan, and porcini from Italy. And I was grateful for all of it.

After a year and a half I lost my work permit and had to return home to Peru. Fresh off my Lutèce experience, I started working with two of the biggest Peruvian chefs at the time, Rafael Osterling and Gastón Acurio. I worked hard—no job was too small or humble, and if the chef asked me to clean the refrigerators many times over, I would. From Friday to Sunday I worked with Rafael at a beach café that was doing fusion cuisine that mixed Asian, Mediterranean, and Peruvian flavors. He gave me the authority to do whatever I wanted in the kitchen, as long as it followed his eclectic style of cooking. It was a fun and educational experience. From Monday through Friday I worked at Astrid y Gastón, which at the time was still leaning towards French cooking. Gradually, Gastón started introducing Peruvian dishes like *lomo saltado* to the menu and started to Peruvianize everything, such as replacing mayonnaise with *huancaina*, a spicy, creamy sauce from the Andes. I didn't completely understand it at the time; I still had this illusion of French superiority in my mind and I wasn't ready to part with it. Yet at the same time I could appreciate that Gastón was building something different. I'm very grateful to this day to have witnessed that process from the beginning and to have been able to watch an empire being built as he rallied the entire country around our food.

I still felt that there was more for me to see abroad, and after six months in Lima, I got a work permit in London. I spent the following three years there, working in different restaurants, including in The Four Seasons. It was there that I had the urge to experience something new, so I went to Asia. I spent three months traveling in Thailand, then I *staged* at a Chinese restaurant in The Four Seasons in Singapore. I saw the Chinese cooks making dim sum and was impressed with their skill level, as they had spent years honing their craft; in contrast, I was really bad at it. It helped to disabuse me of the notion that the fine-dining experience had to be superior. It had a big impact on me. Why was I trying to compete with them when they had a lifetime immersed in this culture? This wasn't a question of just my trying to make Chinese food, but also French or Japanese. I began to think more and more of Peru and its culinary heritage.

Peruvian food was starting to have an impact. Every time I went home I could see that the restaurants were getting better. And not just that: Peruvian ingredients and dishes were popping up everywhere. I saw *ollucos* in Europe, and quinoa in the United States. Daniel Boulud was making ceviche and Raymond Blanc was making *tiradito*. The culinary world was changing.

After another stop in London, Gastón hired me to be the head chef of Astrid y Gastón in Bogotá. It took two years to open and when it finally did I struggled: It was difficult to cook Peruvian food outside of Peru. We had one of the most amazing kitchens I'd ever seen, but I was used to the access to fish we had in Peru. We lacked the produce in Bogotá to make it work. After a year I moved to Madrid to help open another branch of Astrid y Gastón. It was a tough position, as Peruvian food hadn't taken off there quite yet. We might as well have been cooking Icelandic cuisine. Though we had a good structure of flavors, the food costs were high, because back then Peruvian ingredients were not nearly as accessible there as now. Even though the restaurant was packed every night, I felt I was cheating. Why was I cooking Peruvian food in Spain when the availability of the ingredients was so limited? I had to go to the source.

I took a year off to just travel around Peru. I explored the Andes in Cuzco and in Huaraz, the Amazon in Pucallpa, and the coast around Chiclayo. I saw how Peruvians enjoyed their local food much like I saw people in Asia embracing their local cuisine. I came across a huge number of ingredients that I had never seen or heard of or cooked with before and I wanted to do something with this biodiversity, but I didn't know how. I knew that these ingredients were only the starting point.

I worked in quite a few restaurants where I never saw the sun, so when I found this old house in Miraflores with a *pacae* tree growing right in the corner, I thought it was the perfect spot to open a restaurant. Since it never rains in Lima, the restaurant could be partially open to the air and no one would have to sweat throughout their shift. It was so close to the sea, too.

The opening of Central was nothing spectacular. We made some noise, but our food was confused. I kept bringing in European ingredients and trying to mix in Thai flavors and things from my experiences abroad: tuna tataki, truffles— I was still trying to find my own way of cooking Peruvian food.

Peru had begun to change dramatically during this time. With a stable and quickly growing economy, new restaurants were opening everywhere and, for the first time, a middle class that could fill these restaurants was emerging. As the international media caught on, journalists started flying to Peru by the planeloads for Mistura, an annual culinary festival in Lima that began in 2008.

Due to some permit issues, we had to close the restaurant for five months. With this break I had time for a maturing process, to regroup and analyze the situation calmly and to really understand what it meant to own a restaurant. During these months, three huge things happened: First, after being away for so long, I had time to rediscover Lima. Second, I became involved with a project to open another restaurant, in a five-star hotel in Cuzco, establishing a real and true connection to that region's culture and nature. And last, but most importantly, I really got to know Pía, now my wife. I had hired her for a position in the hot prep station that required a lot of physical strength after she swore she could handle it. When the restaurant closed, she insisted that she would stay until it opened again. I realized she was just as driven as I was.

Before reopening, Pía and I went into Central together and cleaned out the entire restaurant. As we scrubbed the grime off everything, we talked about how we were going to run Central in a different way. We changed the menu, making it more robust. We tried to be truer to ourselves, more fearless about what anyone else thought. We began to understand the world of the suppliers, producers, and farmers we were working with. We could benefit from their knowledge and we could also help them create a bigger market. We redesigned the website. I realized all areas of the restaurant were important and I needed to have good communication with everyone who worked there. I thought I could just cook and avoid problems outside the kitchen, but I realized that in addition to cooking, I had a team to lead. I began to look at the front of house and really pay attention to how reservations were being taken. Before I didn't really even know what a maître d' did. These, and other changes, big and small, were fundamental in moving the restaurant forward.

We streamlined the process; we hired fewer people and developed a strategic and specific kitchen hierarchy. Service had to handle more information, and be well directed and focused. There was an area for creativity, where we could experiment with unusual ingredients that we were finding around Peru, which would eventually grow into Mater Iniciativa, the research arm of Central. It elevated the costs of the restaurant, but it was necessary. If there were more people invested in thinking about making the menu better, there was no need for special effects, unnecessary decorations, and garnishes that didn't fit. As we collectively focused on building a better experience, it started to feel more like a family.

With the restaurant doing better financially and everyone happy, I started to think about the next steps. Well before we opened, when I was traveling around Peru after being away for so long, I began to think about a research arm of the restaurant that could explore Peru's biodiversity. I knew it was important, but as a cook I didn't know where to start. This is where my sister Malena got involved. Trained as a doctor, she had just returned to Lima from living in San Diego and was about to take a new job. I told her that if she could help me straighten out the administration part of the restaurant, she could also operate the research arm, which we called Mater Iniciativa.

We soon learned that many of the nature books that have been written had their limitations. For instance, they would call *cushuro*, spherical bacteria found in mountain lakes, seaweed. Despite the endless diversity, there was little formal information out there on what was—and wasn't—edible. We couldn't wait for the ingredients to come to us, we had to go to them—we had to travel.

It became an emotional, transformative experience to find ingredients in their native habitat. Seeing wild cacao beans, or Amazonian fish eating fruit that had fallen into the water, was unbelievable. Little by little we expanded our reach. We found more people who appreciated what we were doing and who were willing to help us. It still wasn't clear to us exactly what we were going to achieve, but we knew that we were going in the right direction.

We had to create a structure where I could leave the restaurant for a few days at a time to travel around Peru on research trips. We had to separate Mater from the restaurant and put together the right team—an interdisciplinary group of specialists, ranging from forest engineers to anthropologists. The kitchen needed to wait until all of the research was ready, until we were done with a particular ingredient, before trying to pull it into the menu.

In structuring the menu, we began thinking about someone coming to Peru for the first time. What were they expecting? Were they aware of this tremendous biodiversity, and how could they have a better connection to it than just experiencing something they have never tasted before? How could we have them explore the country with us? We compiled a database of everything we were discovering and we began to think about a way to communicate all of these different microclimates, all of these unique ingredients, and the extremities of their settings through our food.

We thought of Moray, a series of circular agricultural terraces built by the Incas outside of Cuzco. The temperature in the largest, thirty-meter-deep structure can fluctuate as much as fifteen degrees Celsius (59 degrees Fahrenheit) from the top to the bottom, giving each terrace its own microclimate where different types of plants are grown. Each level is its own ecosystem. It is Peru inverted. It inspired us.

We thought of what the ethno-historian and anthropologist John Murra theorized: that the verticality of the Andean system allowed the Andean people to preserve a nucleus of action at a certain altitude, such as a particular mountain, while at the same time keeping other peripheral nuclei at different altitudes, such as the valleys below, to access a variety of different species, crops, or goods.

As we looked at all the variables of Peru's ecosystems, altitude kept appearing over and over again. Peru's topography is uneven, which may sound chaotic or unwelcoming, and yet it is anything but. This unevenness has an impact on every region, and the wide variation throughout the country is the primary cause of our biodiversity, allowing for all of these different plants and animals to exist and be cultivated.

Once we decided to base our dishes on altitude, with ingredients found together in the same regions, the menu practically wrote itself. It was risky because we were getting into something that was conceptual, but we couldn't sit still. We had to work hard to make these obscure ingredients—things like chaco clay or maca root—seem as familiar in the restaurant as they were in their own ecosystem. Instead of shaving truffles, we shaved *tunta*, a freeze-dried potato.

We don't want to give the impression that our food is strictly Andean. What we find comes from a range of altitudes, many of them, such as the jungles around Paoyhan or the mangroves of Tumbes in the far north, are low-lying altitudes and even, in many cases, below sea level. It's a way of measuring the richness of our biodiversity, from one extreme to another, letting the diner visualize the topography of where our ingredients are coming from.

The more we travel the more we realize how little we know. The natural world in Peru is an astoundingly diverse place. We have barely scratched the surface of what is an enormous, complex world full of intricacies. It's a huge responsibility to communicate this—even more than getting people to eat different things. We have been working to build human relationships through care and trust. We believe that the only way to really become connected is to get to know our people, to try and understand their vision and lifestyle, with an open enough mind to gain some of their wisdom in the process.

In our garden, on the rooftop of Central, we grow a plant called *Oxalis tuberosa*, better known as *oca*. We use the leaves and the flowers as garnishes. They resemble the wood sorrel leaves and stems that are commonly found in thousands of fine-dining restaurants around the world. Yet something is missing. The leaves and flowers are the least interesting part of the plant. What is beneath the earth, hidden from view, is what is important—the roots. But in the lower altitudes of Lima, the roots don't grow into an edible form. They provide just enough sustenance for the stems, leaves, and flowers to grow, but the amount of oxygen in the air and soil components of the coast don't allow the roots to reach full potential. They remain thin and shriveled. Up in the Andes, however, *oca* flourishes—even amid poor soil, extreme altitudes, and unforgiving climates. It's a highly nutritious, almost magical vegetable that comes in a rainbow of colors.

In Lima, we have been a ceviche-eating city-by-the-sea. No one paid any attention to what was on the land behind us. Few places in the world have even a fraction of this abundance. *Eighty-four of the earth's 117 microclimates are here, giving life to an estimated 10 percent of all global species of plants and animals.* Being in Peru and having access to these ingredients is a luxury that we are only beginning to understand as cooks.

We have had to shift our minds away from the city, from everything we thought we knew. From the mountains we can see the entire country. To the north and south the landscape rises and falls, transitioning from wild and windswept grasslands to dense glaciers and jagged peaks. Looking beyond is the Amazon, a vast sea of green forests and twisting rivers. In the other direction we see the coast, barren desert, and valleys splashed with color. Then there is the ocean, an infinite blue merging with the horizon. Each region, each ecosystem, is not defined by borders or numbers, but by its relationship to the world around it. Without one ecosystem there is not the other. Everything is connected.

−25 m • −82 ft

M A R C O N A

MARCONA

The sea becomes more tranquil, the waves, weaker, as the fishermen of San Juan de Marcona return to shore. It's a welcome calm. This bay south of Ica is framed by steep cliffs and huge rock columns protruding from the ocean, sculpted by the intense winds that blow on these shores.

Among the large and imposing rocks where the cold water breaks, we are keeping our eyes out for diver Santiago Canales to surface and show us what he has collected. As we wait, we take the opportunity to forage for different seaweeds, many of which we have heard plenty about. Perhaps it's a lack of curiosity or because culturally we are not accustomed to eating algae, but very few seaweeds are consumed in Peru. Yuyo (*Chondracanthus chamissoi*) is often a garnish, a mere accessory on a plate of ceviche, though most just pick around it.

Some of the algae are attached to stones or lying on the shore. Among the rocks are different species like red rock crabs, sea spiders, red anemones, and starfish moving between the cracks. We came here to see firsthand how these organisms grow and provide food for other species, from plankton to sea lions. In Marcona, a food chain takes place in a very complex ecological context.

Other than in the far north of the country, much of the waters off of the Peruvian coast are cold, brought on by the Humboldt Current, helping make it one of the most productive fishing grounds on earth, though management of fish stock is not always ideal. For example, the Peruvian anchoveta (*Engraulis ringens*), a member of the anchovy family used primarily for fishmeal, is often called "the most heavily exploited fish in world history." Still, sustainable fishing communities can be found here.

The Reserva Nacional San Fernando, just north of Marcona, is an ecological wonder for what it represents in terms of the diversity of marine species. The water is rich in phytoplankton and zooplankton, attracting a variety of crustaceans and fish, forming the foundation of a marine food chain. There are anchoveta, bonito, *caballa*, *jurel*, pejerrey grouper, *pejeperros*, *viejas*, *lenguado*, *chita*, *cavinzas*, *lizas*, and *cojinovas*. There are also octopuses, crabs, scallops, and clams, as well as large stocks of mussels. Yet the diversity here extends far beyond what's beneath the water. In San Fernando Cove is the largest colony of sea lions on the coast. When the pups are born, numerous condors appear. *Guanacos*, a wild species of camelid related to the alpaca, come here from the Andes to feed on the shrubs that grow in the marine humidity. Respecting the limits of this reserve helps all of the ecosystems around it.

We see Santiago's black wetsuit moving toward the shore. As we wade into the cold water to meet him, feeling the strength of the breaking waves, we get a sense of floating among the thousands of organisms that are living around us. From the moment he can stand in the water, Santiago shows us what he managed to catch: sea urchins, snails, *chanque* (abalone), clams, and sea cucumbers. Some rock shrimp are in there too. The richness of the sea seems infinite here.

Approaching a fishing community, and especially the one in Marcona, is no easy task. It is known to be a closed group, with fixed ideas of how things should be handled. The fishermen have a certain distrust of outsiders. They are the children of the children of the old fishermen. They know everything here. They have witnessed the changes in the industry, the indiscriminate harvesting, and how difficult it is to repair nature.

Manuel Milla is our primary contact here. He is a fishing engineer, supervising the community fleet, with a long relationship with the sea. He introduces us to the leaders of the different associations as observers and we tell them about Mater. They explain that their fishing is sustainable, respectful of the seasons and the integrity of the sea. Fishermen, seaweed harvesters, shellfish collectors, and free divers all work together to avoid disturbing the sensitive ecosystem.

It was not always the case though. One of Milla's stories describes a massive layer of sea urchins (*Loxechinus albus*) along the walls of the bay. There was such abundance that they could be consumed for every meal. After extensive and uncontrolled harvesting of this species, those huge populations went through a stage of severe risk. The fishermen decided to impose a ban for four years. Thus, it was possible to recover great numbers of sea urchins, which are now consumed from May to August with full confidence, and today, Marcona remains a place of huge beds of sea urchins.

Arañas de roca

SPIDERS OF THE ROCK

When we arrived at the port of Marcona, one of the things that impressed us the most was these immense rocks protruding from the sea, breaking the waves around them. They are grayish black and irregularly formed, molded by the strong winds and water over many years. While it might not seem so from their forceful stance, they are in a constant state of change. On the plate we interpret these rocks and the sea life that develops around them. The contrasting colors represent the bright orange crabs that climb the rocks and crawl across the bottom of the surrounding dark water, as well as the edible algae that live there, too.

Serves 20

Crab Broth Reduction	Crab shells, 1 kg Tomatoes, 4, chopped Onion, 1 Garlic, 2 cloves Salt	• Place the crab shells in a large pot and cover with 4 L of water. Bring to a boil over medium–high heat, skimming the scum that floats to the surface. Reduce the heat so the stock cooks at a lively simmer. Add the tomatoes, onion, and garlic, and let the stock simmer and cook down for about 1 hour. Season the stock to taste with salt and cook until the liquid is reduced by one-half of the original volume. Remove from the heat, strain through a fine-mesh strainer, cool, and refrigerate until needed.
Shrimp Heads Reduction	Shrimp heads and shells, 500 g Olive oil, 100 ml Cilantro (coriander), 100 g Onion, 1, chopped Celery, ½ stalk, chopped Garlic, 2 cloves Salt	• Rinse the shrimp heads and shells under cold running water and drain. In a large stockpot, heat the oil over medium high heat until hot. Add the shells and heads and cook, stirring, for 6 minutes, until the shells and heads put on some color. Add 2 L of water, the cilantro, onion, celery, garlic, and salt to taste, and, over high heat, bring the stock to a boil. Skim any scum that floats to the surface. Reduce the heat to medium–low and continue to cook at a slow simmer until the stock is flavorful, 45 minutes to 1 hour. Remove from the heat, strain through a fine-mesh strainer, cool, and refrigerate until needed.

→ recipe continues on next page

Arañas de roca

SPIDERS OF THE ROCK

Serves 8

Sweet Potato and Crab Galleta	Sweet potato purée, 300 g Crab Broth Reduction (page 28), 30 ml Shrimp Heads Reduction (page 28), 20 ml Corn oil, for deep-frying	• Preheat the oven to 130°C (266°F). Line a 43 x 31 cm (17 x 12–inch) baking sheet with a silicone mat. • In a bowl, mix together the sweet potato purée, crab reduction, and shrimp reduction. Spread the mixture on the lined baking sheet to about a 5 mm (¼-inch) thickness. Cut the mixture into 24 (5 x 5 cm/2 x 2-inch) pieces. Bake for 30 minutes until baked through and firm. • Meanwhile, in a heavy-bottomed pot, heat the oil to 180°C (356°F). • Carefully transfer the baked galletas from the oven to the hot oil, and deep-fry for 5 seconds, or until crispy.
Tiger's Milk	Celery, 100 g, chopped White onion, 100 g, chopped Garlic, 2 cloves, peeled Peeled fresh ginger, 3 g Cilantro (coriander) stems, 100 g, crushed *Ají limo* pepper, 4 g Fresh key lime juice, from 1 kg key limes Sea water ice cubes, 200 g Grouper belly, 30 g *Yuyo*, 50 g Salt	• In a blender, combine the celery, onion, garlic, ginger, and 200 ml water and blend until smooth. Combine the mixture with the cilantro stems and *ají limo* pepper and refrigerate for 1 hour. Strain and discard the solids. • In a blender, combine the mixture with the lime juice, ice cubes, salt, grouper belly, *yuyo*, and salt to taste and blend until smooth. Strain the mixture through a fine-mesh sieve. Refrigerate until ready to use.
Assembly	Raw *lapas*, 50 g Tiger's Milk (above) Chancaca, 20 g *Yuyo* tips, 20 g Seaweed, 100 g Sea rocks, 8 *Lapa* shells, 8	• Thinly slice the *lapas* and mix with 4 tablespoons of the tiger's milk. Place 100 ml of the tiger's milk in a siphon with 2 charges. • In a saucepan, combine the *chancaca* and 60 ml water and heat until the *chancaca* is melted. Slightly paint the *yuyos* with the melted *chancaca* and set aside on a dry place for about 3 hours until galletas are solid and not sticky. • Divide the sliced *lapas* among the galletas, and use the siphon to top with the tiger's milk. Garnish with the painted *yuyo* tips. • Line 8 plates with seaweed, sea rocks, and *lapa* shells. Place 3 finished galletas on top of each plate and serve.

←recipe starts on previous page

Marcona

Pulpo en su coral

OCTOPUS IN ITS CORAL

Imagine a camouflaged octopus. This dish is all about that sense of place, of where the octopus lives. When the fishermen in Peru go to look for this octopus, it's usually blending in with its environment by hiding under a rock, sometimes a piece of brain coral covered with algae.

We make a cracker with local rice from the coast and dye it with squid ink. It's important that we extract the squid ink ourselves, otherwise it's hard to tell where it came from or how it was obtained. This cracker represents the body of the octopus. We take an algae that is local to the octopus; the algae (*Colpomenia sinuosa*) in Peru is called *alga cerebro*—or sea bubble—because of its bubbly shape. We purée and then fry it, and in yet another play on the name, shape it into the brain coral.

We have many ways of cooking octopus. It's good to think, foremost, about freshness and flavor, but also it's important to understand what we want to achieve on the plate. With that I can determine how I am going to cook it, what I'm going to cook it with, and for how long. Do I want a more concentrated flavor? Should the octopus be soft, semisoft, or semihard? Do I want it to have a crispy exterior and be soft on the inside or tender throughout?

Here, the octopus tentacles are hidden beneath many textures and layers, as if they are peeking out of the algae and coral—we want to sense its movement under the coral, and obtain the greatest amount of flavor. To achieve this, we cook the octopus until it's semisoft, keeping its flavors concentrated. We then reduce the broth in a second cooking of the same octopus, sacrificing the crispy exterior, which can be found elsewhere in the dish with the cracker.

→ recipe continues on next page

Marcona

Pulpo en su coral

OCTOPUS IN ITS CORAL

Serves 8

Costeño Rice	Costeño rice, 200 g Fresh squid ink, 100 g	• In a pot, combine the rice with water to cover (the water should almost reach the top of the pot). Bring to a boil, then reduce the heat to low, cover, and simmer until the rice is tender. Remove from the heat and stir in the squid ink. Let the rice cool, then roll the squid ink rice on a sheet of plastic wrap (clingfilm) into 4 to 5 cylinders, about 5 cm (2 inches) in diameter. Freeze until solid.
Octopus	Octopus, 2 kg Sargassum algae, 30 g Onion, 1, thickly sliced Garlic, 1 head Celery, 1 stalk, roughly chopped Corn oil, 10 ml	• In a large pot, combine the octopus with water to cover. Bring to a boil, reduce the heat to low, add the algae, onion, garlic, and celery, and simmer, uncovered, for 1 hour 30 minutes, or until the liquid has been reduced by half. Remove from the heat and let the octopus cool in the pot to room temperature. Strain and set aside half of the liquid for the next step. Discard the algae, onion, garlic, and celery.
Sea Bubble Cracker	Sea bubble algae, 300 g Octopus bath (above), 50 ml Egg whites, 120 g Potato starch, 30 g	• In a pot, combine the sea bubble algae with water to cover. Bring to a boil, reduce the heat to low, and simmer for 5 hours, uncovered, until soft. Blend the mixture with the reserved octopus broth until a smooth paste forms. • In a clean, dry bowl, whip the egg whites until stiff peaks form; using a spatula, gently fold in the algae paste until combined. Using your hands, shape the mixture into uneven spheres, about 7 cm (2 3/4 inches) in diameter on a dehydrator tray, and dehydrate for 5 hours at 70°C (158°F).
Assembly	*Yuyo*, for serving	• When ready to serve, preheat the oven to 110°C (230°F). Slice the frozen rice across into 20 x 3 cm (7¾ x 1¼-inch) thin slices and bake on a baking sheet for 15 minutes, or until dry and crispy. • Heat a large griddle pan until hot. Place the octopus on the griddle and cook for 1 minute on each side until crispy. Transfer to a cutting board and cut into small pieces. • To serve, place the octopus in a dish and cover with the sea bubble cracker, then top with the *yuyo*.

← recipe starts on previous page

Cosecha y recolección

The name of this dish is kind of an analogy between the crops grown in the soil and what is collected from the sea. Both lettuce and algae are commonplace, growing in great abundance: one on land, the other in the ocean. While lettuce is found in every supermarket, algae is not; even though it contains a wealth of nutrients. The clams are set in the space between the two leaves as if they are being gathered in the seas off the southern coast.

Serves 6

Sargassum algae, 200 g, finely chopped
Clams, 12
Tiger's Milk (page 30), 100 g
Creole lettuce, 1 head, separated into leaves
Sea snail shells, 6

- In a pot, combine the sargassum with water to cover. Bring to a boil, reduce the heat to low, and simmer, uncovered, for 5 hours, or until soft.
- Line a 43 x 31 cm (17 x 12–inch) baking sheet with a silicone mat. Blend the 180 g of the algae (reserve the rest) with its liquid until smooth. Spread the purée on the baking sheet and dry for 2 hours at room temperature.
- Clean and shuck the clams and thinly slice the clam meat; reserve 6 shells. Cover with the tiger´s milk for 10 seconds, and top with the remaining sargassum.
- Heat a grill to high heat. Wrap 10 clam slices in each lettuce leaf and place on the grill, flipping and grilling the wrapped lettuce ball for 5 minutes, or until the clam is cooked through.
- To serve, place the grilled lettuce on the clam shell and the sargassum cracker on the sea snail shell.

M
A
N
G
L
A
R

MANGLAR

With its tangle of roots rising out of the water, the mangrove forest is impenetrable, offering a secure home for many species, out of the reach of various predators. The earth beneath them is muddy—a dark, gray, and mysterious place. While it might seem inhospitable, the mangrove is layered with deposits of organic matter, such as leaves that fall and decompose, nourishing countless species of crustaceans and mollusks, setting into motion an extensive food chain.

Off the coast of Tumbes and Piura in the far north of Peru, the water is warmer, resulting in a remarkably different set of marine species than of the colder waters of the Humboldt Current that runs along much of our coast. The water is brackish where the sea meets the streams from the mountains, the home of the mangrove ecosystem, redistributing the organic matter and sediment, and regulating the salinity.

The mangroves are the habitat for more than forty species of plants, predominantly species of red mangrove (*Rhizophora mangle* and *Rhizophora harrisonii*), which, as the tide brings in more nutrients, grow almost beyond measure. Within these mangroves also live one of our most emblematic species, *conchas negras* (*Anadara tuberculosa*), a black clam that lives buried beneath the mud, amid the roots of the mangroves at depths of 10 to 30 centimeters (4 to 12 inches), filtering nutrients with their gills.

In Zarumilla, the mangrove covers an area of more than 2,900 hectares (11 square miles). The value of this ecosystem lies not only in its biological diversity, but also culturally, as its resources provide food and a source of income for the locals.

We arrived at Puerto 25 that morning from Tumbes. We are covered in repellent against the threat of being besieged by hundreds of insects, and are wearing wide-brimmed hats to protect against the intense heat of a sun, which feels deceptively cool when you're in a fast-moving boat.

The port is a meeting point for the fishermen and clam diggers in the area. Many of them have been coming here since the port was built, some forty years ago. They are chatting, preparing for the day's work, milling about. A group of eight to ten men, ranging from about thirty to sixty years old, are watching us curiously, tilting their heads as they stare. It's clear we're not a group of tourists, so they're wondering what we're doing.

Aldo Durand and Guillermo Montoya are two biologists who work with surrounding communities, to ensure that the preservation of species is respected and that the areas around the sanctuary are not changed, since their impact on the protected area is quite significant. They introduce us to the fishermen. We're eager to meet them, to learn more about what they do. "This is our life," says one, in a way that signals it is more than just their livelihood. Their activities are rooted in their culture and he makes clear that they respect the efforts to preserve the sanctuary. They realize its richness can only exist when the ecosystem is healthy. *Conchas negras* are so emblematic to the port, yet they had been overharvested for so long that the fishermen have seen what happens when the population is exploited. A seasonal ban from mid-February to the end of March has been put in place in hopes of increasing the population.

The Tumbes mangrove area was named a protected area in 1978 as a precaution against the growing shrimp industry, and has been a national sanctuary since 1988. The shrimp industry, overfishing, and overharvesting of the shellfish are still major threats to the ecosystem, though climate change is an additional cause for concern. Despite the shifting nature of the mangroves, they're more fragile than they seem. During the El Niño phenomenon, heavier rainfall increases the flow of the river, pushing out marine waters and decreasing the salinity. This kills off many species, including *conchas negras*. With each El Niño the weather patterns are more and more extreme and the effects are more and more devastating.

Huddled together in a small boat we steer into a swirl of waters flowing from the Zarumilla River and a few small streams from Peruvian territory, and the Jubones and Arenillas Rivers from Ecuador. The water is greenish, with dark patches, but as you move closer to the mangroves it becomes blackish-brown. From time to time we stop to soak up the nature around us. Orange and green leaves contrast with the muted tones of these twisted trees. Bright red crabs, with the slightest movement, stand out amid the roots and mud. Every gust of air sees a heron flying. Frigate birds puff out their red pouches, and a huge salamander crawls on the branch of a tree.

On the shore we are expecting to step into sand. Instead, it feels like a carpet of shells, the remains of all of the many species of bivalves that live here. It hurts to step on them. Through the clear water, bands of color form in the glare of the midday sun. On the boat, Francisco Silva, a *conchero* and son of a fisherman, teaches us how to dig in the mud of mangroves to find conchas negras. He covers himself with protective gear to prevent scratches and tears as he digs through the mud. A hood covers his face revealing only his eyes, as if he's a ninja. His ears are covered too, in case they should be poked by the mangrove branches. Cotton is wrapped around each of the fingers of his left hand, while red cotton sleeves cover his arms from his armpit down to the heel of his hands, with holes for his fingers to slip out.

His legs sink into the soft soil of the mangrove mud, almost to the tops of his rubber boots. In his right hand he has a mesh bag to keep the clams he finds. He bends over and quickly slides his entire arm into the mud. Through intuition and experience, he knows exactly where and how, because after a minute, four or five shells are held in his fingers and released into the mesh bag he holds in his right hand. Each collection day he can amass up to 150 clams, but he must pay special attention to size, which must exceed 4.5 centimeters (1¾ inches) in diameter, or he has to put them back.

We learn and feel. For us, burying our arms into these unknown textures is completely alien. How strange it is to come across these rough, hard-textured shells in this soft, squishy substance. There's a feeling that the mud will completely suck you in, as if it's alive.

Reflection on Raw Seafood

In the first chapters we see examples of how to work with clams, conchas negras from the mangroves, grouper belly, and scallops—all of it raw. The truth is that whenever we think about new dishes that will involve seafood, we always prefer it in its raw form—even if it is hard, even if it is gummy, chewy, or rubbery, we still prefer the raw over the cooked. It's vital to work with it alive, to get a sense of the creature in its natural state. On first impression it might be more accommodating to the diner to give seafood a traditional preparation to ensure a pleasurable texture and taste, but a dimension of rawness is a part of our identity. It's an imprint on our memory of the freshness of the ingredients from the sea. To live so close to the sea, to smell it and capture its essence—the entirety of the flavor of each component is what we try to communicate in each dish.

Lengua piedra

STONE TONGUE

This dish represents some of the things we found living together along the northern coast, a place of contrasting sweet, sour, and salty flavors. The *barquillos*, a type of chiton, sort of licks the algae of the rocks and the meat looks almost like a tongue. We serve them on a plate of frozen shells, mimicking the cold sea where they came from.

Serves 4

Sea water, 500 ml
Orange prickly pear, 1, juiced
Miel de Palo, 20 g
Salty fingers, 3, stems
  and tips separated
Barquillos, 4 unshucked

- In a pot, combine the sea water, prickly pear juice, and *miel de palo*. Bring to a boil, then reduce the heat to low and add the salty fingers' stems and *barquillos*, and simmer for 1 minute. Remove from the heat and set aside to cool.
- Once the *barquillo* meat has absorbed all of the flavors—after 10 minutes—pick the meat out of the shells and clean it (keep the shells for plating). In a bowl, place the shells with water to cover and put them in the freezer; when it is completely frozen use this dish to plate.
- Slice the salty fingers' tips and place them raw just on top of the *barquillos'* "tongues." Place everything on top of frozen shells and serve.

Lengua piedra

Suelo de mangle

MANGROVE SOIL

The pepino melon is a unique fruit that grows at the same sea level as the mangrove roots, just a bit above the water. Sometimes it grows so low that it can even almost be looking at a clam. Translating to cucumber melon, the name correctly suggests it's like a cross between a cucumber and a melon: slightly sweet, with pale yellow skin marked by black streaks. Like both cucumber and melon, this hybrid is fresh tasting, mild, and contains lots of water. We decided to include this particular fruit in a preparation that wouldn't normally match it with other sweet flavors. It may even sound odd to pair it with seafood, especially razor clams—which, when in season, are like gifts sent from heaven. And while it's rare that we find fruit and shellfish that go well together, with the variety of fruit growing in the places we visit, the pairing deserves experimentation.

Sometimes you just have to work on the proportions, test the ripeness, play with fermentation, or try a lot of different options. We cover the plate with foam made from the water of the razor clams and that gives it a stronger taste of the sea. It's important that we add algae, too, which helps to control the sweetness of the melon.

Serves 8

Razor clams, 16
Avocado oil, 30 ml
Sea salt
Pepino melons, 3
Borage leaves and stems

- Clean and shuck the clams, then cut each clam into thirds, reserving the juices.
- In a small saucepan, combine the clam juices, avocado oil, and salt to taste. Bring to a boil, reduce the heat to low, and simmer until the liquid is of syrupy consistency.
- Peel 1 pepino melon and thinly shave. Juice the remaining melons. Blend the pepino melon juice with the clam juice reduction until foamy. Set aside.
- Place 2 razor clams per person on a plate, cover with melon shavings, and add the melon–clam sauce. Top with the borage leaves and stems.

Manglar

Roca de manglar

ROCK OF THE MANGROVES

To convey a sense of place from the mangroves is quite a complex process. You can start with the salty sea, the river water, the muddy soil, the mangrove roots, or the low-hanging fruits. We don't feel comfortable in saying that a single ingredient is a dish. Rather a dish is the sum of three factors: a good understanding of the ingredient, creativity, and sensitivity to the world around it. When we travel to the mangroves, our primary objective is to find *conchas negras*. However, we search, harvest, and experiment with them knowing all of their baggage: the restrictions, bans, and environmental concerns. Therefore, we serve the *conchas negras* buried, just the way we found them.

Serves 8

Salicornia, 160 g
Conchas negras, 40
Grated sweet lime zest, from 2 limes
Sea salt
Heavy (double) cream, 90 ml
Green oxalis stems and leaves, 400 g
Purslane, 100 g

- Cut all the salicornias into two parts (stems and tips).
- Clean and shuck the clams, reserving their juices. Set aside the clams in the refrigerator.
- In a pot, combine the reserved clam juice, half of the salicornia stems, sweet lime zest, and salt to taste. Bring to a boil, then reduce to a simmer and cook, uncovered, until the liquid is reduced to half its original volume. Remove from the heat and refrigerate until cold.
- In a clean, chilled bowl, combine the clam reduction with the cream and whip until soft peaks form. Set aside.
- Prepare a charcoal grill. Grill the other half of salicornia stems over the coals until well charred. Transfer to a blender and pulverize to a fine powder. Set aside.
- Spread the salicornia tips and 200 g of green oxalis leaves on a dehydrator tray and dehydrate at 40°C (104°F) for 3 hours, then pulverize them in a blender until the texture of coarse salt. Set aside.
- On plates, spoon the clam cream over the clams; they should be submerged in the cream. Dust with burnt salicornia powder and salicornia "salt". Top with purslane as well as the remaining oxalis leaves and stems. Serve immediately.

85 m · 279 ft

O
R
I
L
L
A

ORILLA

Our intimate relationship with the sea always makes us look a little closer at the shore. Our coast is arid, a huge space of blue sky and sand dunes, and flora and fauna that are rarely seen. Ica's desert appears monochromatic and desolate, with the wind picking up a fine dust and boiling sand that smacks you in the face. Yet in the desert there is much more life than you might expect. It's an ecosystem all unto itself, and in it exists a tree.

We were brought here in large part for the *huarango*, a variety of *Prosopis*, called *limensis*, a carob tree. It grows slowly and can live for over 1,000 years. As tall as 18 meters (60 feet), with a twisted, gnarled trunk, it survives in dry soils like this: places of intense heat, rapid rates of evaporation, little rainfall, and winds of great speeds. Using its long, lateral roots, the tree absorbs whatever scarce rainwater reaches the ground, and extends as far as 50 meters (165 feet) below ground to reach the groundwater.

The *huarango* makes other plant life possible in this hyper-arid, fragile environment. Its shade allows other plants to grow and animals to take refuge. The trees are great at replenishing nitrogen in the soil and at reducing salinity and storing water that is available for other plant systems. The trees are an island of moisture and fertility, the keystone of this desert ecosystem, underpinning the biodiversity around it.

We find *huarangos* seemingly floating on the dunes. Surrounding them is more life: Fruit-producing cacti like *ulluquite* (*Neoraimondia arequipensis*) share the landscape, as do slender-billed finches (*Xenospinus concolor*) and owls, plus native plants like *tecoma* (*Tecoma arequipensis*), *toñuz* (*Pluchea chingollo*), *palo brea* (*Parkinsonia praecox*), *espino* (*Acacia macracantha*), and *lucraco* (*Waltheria ovata*), most of which have medicinal uses.

In the kitchen we are mostly interested in the fruit that the *huarango* produces. The slightly curved yellow seed pods grow up to 28 centimeters (11 inches) in length. The seeds contain a high percentage of fiber (more than 70 percent) and are often ground into flour to be used for baking. Already sweet, no sugar needs to be added.

In Samaca, we are taught the process for obtaining the syrup. The pods are boiled for hours in huge pots over a wood fire of fallen eucalyptus trees. Afterwards, the pods are strained and pressed by machines that exert strong pressure to extract this very thick, sweet syrup. Some local people simply evaporate the mixture until it has a very dense consistency.

Pre-Colombian cultures have been utilizing the *huarango's* resources for thousands of years. (It was even depicted in the Nazca Lines, a series of ancient geoglyphs etched into the desert in southern Peru.) There is evidence that the fruit was turned into powders, syrups, and fermented drinks. The fallen leaves were used as fertilizer, while other leaves and branches fed animals like alpacas and guanacos. The wood itself was used for construction and ritual objects.

That ancient civilizations always treated the environment with the utmost respect is a misconception; that wasn't always the case. They could mess things up, too. The Nazca built a great civilization amid this desert environment for about five hundred years, but then they became greedy. As their population swelled they began to cut down the *huarango* forests for firewood and to plant more crops. Deforestation created an imbalance in the ecosystem and when a massive El Niño event around 500 AD unleashed heavy rainfall in the Andes that then flooded the coast, it was no longer able to handle the effects. Crops and buildings washed away. When the Wari, a civilization that predated the Incas, came down from the highlands they picked the Nazca apart.

Spanish chroniclers referred to the presence of forests of *huarangos* in the desert between Pisco and Ica all the way to the town of Nazca. Patches still exist, yet today deforestation has taken its toll. The population of *huarangos* continues to decline, due to continued growing demands for firewood and agricultural lands. Winds have blown away the topsoil and the ecosystem is a fraction of what it once was. We have learned none of the lessons of the past and the effects of each El Niño continue to be devastating. However, there is a tiny sliver of hope. Efforts are underway to reforest the *huarango* throughout the region and to raise awareness among locals on the many benefits of preserving the *huarangos'* ecosystem. Maybe—just maybe—by serving a sweetener made from huarango at Central, and letting the general public know about sustainable uses that promote keeping these trees in the ground, we are helping, too.

Fósil de concha

SCALLOP FOSSIL

We were on our way back from Samaca, an organic farm in the Ocucaje Desert, where we were looking for *huarango* trees and exploring desert ecosystems. We found these incredible species of plants that could survive with very little water. We noticed a few men digging on the side of the road. They were removing stones, huge slabs of rock, and one caught my sister Malena's attention. It was the perfect shape of a scallop, yet we were so far from the sea, so it couldn't be a scallop. Or *could* it? We were in the middle of the desert, full of shifting sand dunes—the very opposite of the ocean— and this fossilized shell caught us off guard. Yet, in that very spot, tens of millions of years ago, scallops once lived. Maybe, if we dug deep enough into the sand, we'd find water again.

This fossilized scallop shell got us thinking about the history of this landscape; about how old it was and how we could communicate that on the plate. *Tumbo*, a relative of passion fruit, immediately came to mind. When the Spanish first made contact with Peru, it is written that they saw natives eating a crude form of ceviche, using the juice of *tumbo* (limes hadn't yet been imported by the Spanish). Thinking of the concept of time in a more abstract way—the millions of years that have passed since the scallops were living here—we soak the scallop in the tumbo for several hours rather than just a few seconds as traditionally would befit a ceviche. We continue with another long, slow preparation by boiling *pata de gallo*, a twig-like algae, completely transforming its structure into a sticky gum, which we then dry before deep-frying. The scallop gets a cane syrup glaze, but it never touches heat. Everything stays cold. When it's served, directly on a fossilized scallop shell, I like to think that you really get a sense of this ancient sea.

→ recipe continues on next page

Fósil de concha

SCALLOP FOSSIL

Serves 4

Yuyo, 200 g
Sea lettuce, 100 g
Tiger's Milk (page 30), 200 ml
Tumbo juice, 30 ml
Scallops, 4
Pacae Crystals (page 234), 20 g
Pata de gallo algae, 10 g
Olive oil

- In a large saucepan, combine the yuyo, sea lettuce, and 3 L water. Bring to a boil, reduce the heat to low, and simmer, uncovered, for 5 hours, or until yuyo is soft.
- Line a 43 x 31 cm (17 x 12-inch) baking sheet with a silicone mat. Transfer the algae mixture to a blender and purée until smooth. Spread the purée on the lined baking sheet and let sit at room temperature for 2 hours, until dry. Cut the dried seaweed into 5 cm (2-inch) squares, or break it into free-form pieces of similar size.
- In a bowl, combine the tiger's milk and tumbo juice. Place the scallops in the marinade and refrigerate, covered, for 3 hours.
- Melt the pacae crystals at low temperature in a double boiler (bain marie).
- Bring a medium-size pot filled with water to a boil over high heat and blanch the pata de gallo algae for 5 seconds, then shock in an ice bath.
- Cover the pata de gallo with a thin coat of the melted pacae crystals, let them dry.
- Heat a large skillet over high heat with just enough oil to cover the bottom of the pan. Add the dried seaweed pieces and sear for about 30 seconds.
- To serve, remove the scallops from the marinade and place over the seaweed. Top with pata de gallo and make a wrap. This is one bite.

← recipe starts on previous page

Cassava Starch

We find *yuca* everywhere in Peru, from the coast to the Andes and the Amazon. It's a special crop, which is why it appears at different altitudes and may be combined with ingredients from multiple regions. We use the starch from the *yuca* (called cassava or tapioca starch) to stabilize our *cristales*, which are our sweeteners. It works perfectly in maintaining their structure.

Makes 110 g

White cassava, 1 kg

- Peel the cassava and then pass through a juicer. Pass the juice through a Superbag twice.
- Line a dehydrator tray with a silicone mat mat. Pour the liquid into a tray, place in a dehydrator, and dehydrate at 63°C (146°F) for 14 hours, or until it becomes a dry block.
- Transfer the block to a food processor and pulse until a fine powder forms. Keep in a sealed, dry container for up to 2 weeks.

Diversidad de maíz

DIVERSITY OF MAIZE

The role of farmers has been central to the diversification of maize in the country. The wide range is in part because of our ecological diversity, but mutation, hybridization, acclimatization, and selection has been at the hands of the farmers themselves. The careful management of these field varieties represents enormous challenges. Here we wanted to illustrate them, revealing everything about the diversity and the full use of the ingredient. We chose six varieties of maize, all originating from the coast.

To make corn broth ceviche we use a varietal from Tumbes, which is almost exclusive to this northern region. With mealy white or yellow kernels, it is sourced from the hot and arid coastal desert.

Although maize tends to be a garnish in ceviche, here the concept is inverted. Inside the cup is a liquid corn ceviche—or a maize *leche de tigre*—with all the ingredients of a ceviche, but instead of fish, it's the maize that unites all the flavors.

Serves 20

Corn Leaves Stock	Coruca corn leaves, 400 g Chancayano amarillo corn leaves, 400 g Chaparreño corn leaves, 400 g Pardo corncobs, 400 g Perla corncobs, 250 g Purple corncobs, 250 g	• Using a blow torch, singe all the corn leaves. In a large pot, combine the leaves with 4 L water and bring to a boil with all the types of corncobs. Reduce the heat, and simmer, uncovered, for 30 minutes. Remove from the heat and set aside.
Corn Broth Ceviche	Corn Leaves Stock (above), 1 L *Tumbo* fruit, 2, pulp only *Ají amarillo* paste, 50 g Fresh ginger, 1 piece (1 cm/½ inch) Garlic, 2 cloves, peeled White onion, 1, chopped Chancayano amarillo corn kernels, 25 g Cilantro (coriander) stems, 30 g Corn oil, 20 ml	• In a pot, bring the corn leaves stock to a boil and reduce it to 300 ml. Remove from the heat and refrigerate until cold. • In a blender, combine the stock reduction with the *tumbo* pulp, the *ají amarillo* paste, ginger, garlic, white onion, corn kernels, and cilantro stems. Add the corn oil and blend until the mixture is fully emulsified; pass through a fine chinois, pour into a squeeze bottle, and refrigerate.

→ recipe continues on next page

Diversidad de maíz

DIVERSITY OF MAIZE

Yellow Corn Cake

Chancayano amarillo corn kernels, 200 g
Chaparreño corn kernels, 200 g
Pardo corn kernels, 200g
Perla corn kernels, 100 g
Ají amarillo paste, 80 g
White onion, ¼
Corn Leaves Stock (page 68),
Cilantro (coriander) 1 bunch
Huarango Crystals (page 235), 20 g
Corn oil, 5 ml
Flaky sea salt

- In a skillet, sear the 4 types of corn kernels with the *ají amarillo* paste and the onion, then add just enough of the corn stock to cover, and cook until the liquid has been absorbed. Add the cilantro just to infuse for 15 minutes; then remove and discard.
- Transfer the mixture to a blender with the *huarango* crystals, corn oil, 500 ml water, and flaky salt and blend until smooth. Pass through a fine-mesh sieve. Line a 43 x 31 cm (17 x 12-inch) rimmed baking sheet with a silicone mat. Using a spatula, evenly spread the purée on the lined sheet. Let the purée sit for 2 hours until congealed; using a 1 cm (⅓-inch) ring cutter, punch out rounds. Refrigerate until needed.

Purple Corn Cake

Purple corn kernels, 300 g
Chancayano amarillo corn kernels, 250 g
Pardo corn kernels, 250 g
Perla corn kernels, 150 g
White onion, ¼
Corn Leaves Stock (see p. 68), 1 L
Cilantro (coriander) 1 bunch
Corn oil, 15 ml
Salt
Huarango Crystals (page 235), 20 g

- In a skillet, sear the 4 types of corn kernels with the onion, then add just enough of the corn stock to cover, and cook until the liquid has been absorbed. Add the cilantro just to infuse for 15 minutes; then remove and discard.
- Transfer the mixture to a blender with the *huarango* crystals and blend until smooth. Pass through a fine-mesh sieve. Line a 43 x 31 cm (17 x 12-inch) rimmed baking sheet with a silicone mat. Using a spatula, evenly spread the purée on a lined sheet. Let the purée sit for 2 hours until congealed; using a 1 cm (⅓-inch) ring cutter, punch out rounds. Refrigerate until needed.

Fried Corn Silk

Corn oil, 1 L
Corn silk, 100 g

- In a heavy pot, heat the oil until it reaches 175°C (347°F). Carefully lower the corn silk into the oil and deep-fry for 2 seconds.

← recipe starts on previous page

Corn Skin Ring

Chancayano amarillo corn purée,
  900 g
Salt, 5 g
Perla corn kernels, 50 g
Ají amarillo paste, 100 g
Pardo corn powder, 200 g
Corn oil, 30 ml

- In a sauté pan, cook the Chancayano corn purée over low heat, stirring constantly, for about 20 minutes, or until golden brown. Season with the salt, remove from the heat, and set aside until cold. Crush until the mixture is almost a powder.
- Using a mortar and pestle, crush the Perla corn. In a pan set over low heat, toast the crushed kernels until golden brown, about 5 minutes.
- In a saucepot, combine the Chancayano amarillo corn purée, *aji amarillo* paste, half of the crushed corn, and salt, and cook over low heat, stirring frequently, for 30 minutes until the mixture resembles a thick dough. Line a 43 x 31 cm (17 x 12–inch) rimmed baking sheet with a silicone mat, and using 5 cm (2–inch) circle stencils, spread the mixture onto the lined sheet. Sprinkle with the remaining toasted Perla corn.

- To serve, cut the corn cakes into round shapes. Stack the cakes alternating the colors to get 5 disks per cylinder. Top each cylinder with the fried corn silk. Pour the corn broth ceviche into a small cylindrical vase, and top with a corn skin ring. Serve the cylinders alongside the corn broth ceviche.

Orilla

Conchas del desierto

SHELLS IN THE DESERT

This dish evokes the desert ecosystem along the arid route south of Lima where our scallops come from—a route of dunes so empty and arid that the smell of the sea and the occasional cactus are the only hints of life that you may encounter.

Serves 4

Prickly Pear Crisps	Prickly pear juice, 200 g	• Line a 43 x 31 cm (17 x 12–inch) dehydrator tray with a silicone mat. In a saucepan, cook the prickly pear juice over medium heat for 10 minutes, or oruntil it thickens to a gel–like consistency. Remove from the heat. Spread the prickly pear gel on the dehydrator tray and dehydrate at 65°C (149°F) for 10 hours, or until crisp. Set the prickly pear crisps aside.
Cactus Crisps	Cactus (prickly pear leaf), 250 g *Pata de gallo* algae, 100 g	• Preheat the oven to 130°C (266°F). Line a 43 x 31 cm (17 x 12–inch) rimmed baking sheet with a silicone mat. • In a blender, purée the cactus stalk with the algae until smooth, then pass through a fine-mesh sieve. Spread the cactus purée on the lined baking sheet and bake in the oven for 20 minutes, or until it is dry and crispy.
Scallops	Scallops (in the shell), 8 Avocado oil, 100 ml *Caigua*, 4	• To clean the scallops, remove from the shells and set the roe aside. Cut the scallops, vertically, into thirds. Set aside. Stir the reserved roe into the avocado oil until emulsified. • In a saucepan, heat 10 ml of the avocado-roe oil over low heat. • Cut the base of the *caigua* all along vertically to facilitate placing on the dish. • Add the *caigua* to saucepan and cook until soft.
Assembly	*Pata de gallo* algae, for garnish	• To serve, place the *caigua* on the plate and cover with the pieces of scallops, pass the torch on the scallops to singe them a little bit; then top with the cactus crisps and *pata de gallo*.

Gel de cactus

CACTUS GEL

In Peru, we have no tradition of eating cactus. If we see them in our path on the side of the road, they are considered a part of our landscape. However, at Central, we are always interested in collecting some part of the road. Sometimes we find round flowers of different colors, other times fruits, depending on the species. I take advantage of the leaf or the paddle of the cactus, to make gels and thickeners in cold liquids, such as a *leche de tigre* of cactus that was once on the Alturas menu.

Makes 50 g

Cactus paddle, 1 medium

- Peel and scrape the cactus. Place in a bowl, cover, and refrigerate until needed. Cactus gel keeps for 3 days.

Gel de cactus

Infusión solar de maíz morado

SOLAR INFUSION OF PURPLE CORN

Once in a while we put a solar infusion in our nonalcoholic pairing experience at Central. To qualify for a pairing, a drink must originate from the same soil as the dish, and must coexist at the same altitude with the ingredients in the dish. For these infusions, we rely on the energy from the sun. We have a large open kitchen area, which allows us to set out various glass jars filled with different ingredients that are fully exposed to the light of the coastal desert sun. There are many variables, such as temperature, in utilizing this solar energy, though skins and remnants of other preparations that might be used in the infusions also have an effect. The solar infusions may come from the kitchen or cocktail bar and sometimes we use a new ingredient we collected from a new zone during our travels with Mater. We serve these drinks at around 7° to 8°C (44° to 47°F).

Makes 15 (200 ml) bottles

Purple corn, 1 kg, kernels cut off, husks reserved
Corn leaves

- In an 8 L canister, combine the corn husks and kernels with 2 L water. Place the canister in a sunny place and let sit for 3 hours. Then refrigerate for 2 hours until fully chilled. Strain the liquid through a fine-mesh sieve and divide among fifteen 200 ml bottles. Cover the mouths of the bottles with corn leaves and secure with a string. Store, refrigerated, for up to 2 days.

Orilla

Árbol y alga dulce

TREE & SWEET ALGAE

An idea came to me on the last day of a trip searching for *huarango* trees, which are found in high temperatures, sometimes facing the sea. On the way back we stopped for a few hours to rest on the beach, to help restore our bodies after a day of walking in intense heat amidst the dry forest. Our car was already loaded up with *huarango* molasses and dried fruit and pods that had fallen off the trees. We were excited when we saw *pacae* trees near the shore, and in front of us, on the beach, was a shocking amount of algae. I started to think of a cold and refreshing drink made with everything we had around us at that moment.

There was a local hostel nearby, and we asked them for some ice. We climbed a pacae tree and cut down the fruit. We put the ice and peeled pacae "cotton" in a glass along with some algae, and added some *huarango* syrup to sweeten, stirring until the ice, the algae, and the fruit were one—a dense, granita-style drink. The next day, back at Central, we played with this idea as we tend to do. We recreated the experience of the previous day using a Pacojet in our kitchen. This recipe, a sort of sorbet, was the result.

Serves 8

Sea lettuce, 20 g
Yuyo, 50 g
"Cotton" from *pacae* pods, 320 g
Huarango molasses, 30 ml
Huarango wood chips, 300 g
Sea salt

- In a saucepan, bring 600 ml water to a boil, turn off the heat, and add the sea lettuce and *yuyo*. Cover and let the liquid infuse, for 10 minutes. Strain through a fine-mesh sieve. Reserve the liquid and discard the sea lettuce and *yuyo*. Refrigerate the infusion until cold.
- Mix the *pacae* "cotton" with the cold infused water and *huarango* molasses. Using a smoker, cold-smoke the mixture using *huarango* wood chips for 15 minutes and then let it rest, covered, for 1 hour.
- Freeze the mixture and then pass it through the Pacojet. Serve with a pinch of sea salt.

1,600 m • 5,249 ft

BAJO ANDINO

The topography of Lima is mostly brown. The deep blue sea clashing against the brownness of the barren hills of the coastal desert, which stretches from the north of Peru all the way down the coast to Chile, is the first thing you notice upon landing at Jorge Chavez airport. The empty lots are brown and most of the houses are made of brown bricks. Yet in the Rímac, Lurín, and Chillón River Valleys that surround the ever-expanding metropolitan area, the color green dominates.

Agriculture is a tradition in these coastal valleys, dating back an estimated 7,000 years. The fertile soil and stable climate at a range of altitudes allowed for the year-round harvesting of cotton, maize, beans, sweet potatoes, and other vegetables, which helped give rise to civilizations that have left pyramids all over the central coast.

South of Lima, Pachacamac—a sacred archeological complex from 500 years ago—was inhabited by a succession of different cultures, from the Lima and Wari to the Yschma and finally the Incas. Each left temples and buildings more impressive than their predecessors. The site is symbolically located at a point between a lagoon, the mouth of the Lurín River, and the Pacific Ocean. Archeologists have uncovered evidence of alternating periods of severe droughts and floods over a two-thousand-year period, as well as several tsunamis that inundated the site with salt water. When conquistador Pedro Pizarro visited the main temple in 1534, he found a door covered with a cloth with the image of a *Spondylus*, a type of a mollusk, on it. The connection to water has been closely tied to the cycle of life in this dry region, and it continues to be to this day. Heavy rains and droughts tied to increasingly powerful El Niño effects and melting glaciers in the Andes, along with urban expansion, threaten life throughout the region.

From Pachacamac we turn left into the foothills of the Andes, deeper into the Lurín River Valley. Unlike in Lima, the sun is usually shining here. Small, family-owned organic farms dot the landscape. We pass an ancestral farm that grows fruits native to the region—like *lúcuma*, *cherimoya*, and *guanábana*, which have helped define the regional cuisine for thousands of years—before we reach Santa Rosa de Mal Paso where we find the farm of the Silvera family.

The road doesn't reach the farm, so we have to hike along a small stream for fifteen minutes or so. Two black Labradors come out to greet us and lead us to Carmen, the mother, who is complaining about birds picking at the beans and some of the fruits.

"How do you keep them away?" I ask.

"You just have to chase after them and clap your hands," she laughs.

Vermilion flycatchers, tiny bright red birds, hide in the trees, breaking the greenery. On a post hangs a bag filled with *aguardiente* (a crude alcohol distilled from sugarcane) and a thin, long snake that they killed on the property. They call it *ron de culebra*—or snake rum—and Carmen's daughter Doris says they drink it when someone has a fever.

We first met Carmen's other daughter, Diana, at the Bioferia, a Saturday organic market at Parque Reducto in Lima, around the time that Central opened. She has helped the family find a niche, pushing for quality produce, and she encouraged them to make their own compost and biofuel. She's the farm's primary contact at the restaurant and we speak to her often.

During Peru's years of terrorism, waves of farmers from Central Andean regions like Huancavelica and Huánuco migrated to the coast, establishing themselves in these lower Andean valleys, bringing with them traditional farming methods. Diana's father came from Andahuaylas to work for someone who owned a large plot of land here. Eventually, he saved enough money to buy a piece of it.

There's not a single crop that dominates the 1 hectare (2½-acre) farm. A dense ring of banana and avocado trees and tall grasses frame the land, which is crisscrossed with neatly lined rows of different crops like *arracacha*—a yellow or white root vegetable related to carrots—sweet potatoes, *huacatay*, and various wild tomatoes and aromatics.

We walk to the edge of the property where the normally dry riverbed is flowing with water. Narrow channels filled with water have flooded over their borders and have merged together. It's very unusual and the water is rising every day, Doris says. She's afraid that it's going to flood the farm and destroy the crops. There is little that they can do to stop the water; they just have to wait and see.

Palto y las semillas

AVOCADO & SEEDS

The avocado is a way of life in Peru. Everyone always has a few ripe ones in the kitchen. We make this dish only when we get the best avocados in season.

Serves 6

Beet Powder	Beets, 3, peeled	• Preheat the oven to 140°C (285°F). Line a (43 x 31 cm/ 18 x 13–inch) baking sheet with a silicone mat. • Process the beets in a juice extractor, reserving the pulp and the juice. Spread the pulp on the lined sheet and bake at 140°C (285°F) for 1 hour , or until the mixture is half dry. • Remove from the oven and process in the blender. Once pulverized, return to the lined baking sheet and return to the oven until completely dry, about 30 minutes more.
White & Green Lake Algae Crunch	Milk, 50 ml Cassava Starch (page 64), 100g Egg whites, 200 g Salt Dry lake algae, 200 g	• Preheat the oven to 160°C (320°F). Line 2 baking sheets with silicone mats. • In a bowl, stir together milk, cassava starch, egg whites, and a pinch of salt. Divide the dough between 2 bowls and set aside. • Spread the algae on a baking sheet and place in the oven for 10 minutes. Divide in half. (Leave the oven on.) • For the green crunch, purée half of the algae in a blender and mix with one-half of the dough. Spead a thin layer on a lined sheet and bake for 10 minutes, or until dry. • For the white crunch, spread a thin layer of the dough on a lined sheet. Crush the remaining algae with gloved hands and sprinkle over the dough. Bake for 10 minutes, or until dry.
Tamarillo	*Ají amarillo*, 1 *Tamarillos*, 500 g Avocado oil, 60 ml	• Preheat the oven to 200°C (392°F). • In a pot of boiling water, blanch the *ají amarillo*, then cool and peel. • Peel and quarter the *tamarillos* . Arrange on a baking sheet, drizzle with a little avocado oil, and roast in the oven for 20 minutes, until golden brown. • Transfer the *tamarillos* to a blender, add the *ají amarillo*, and blend.
Kiwicha	*Kiwicha*, 20 g Beet juice (reserved from Beet Powder, above) *Annatto* oil, 5 ml Salt	• In a saucepan, combine the *kiwicha* and enough water to cover. Bring to a boil and cook for 9 minutes until al dente. Drain and set aside to cool. • Transfer the *kiwicha* to a bowl and stir in some of the beet juice. Season with *annatto* oil and salt.
Roasted Avocado	Avocados, 3 Salt Avocado oil, 50 ml	• Preheat the oven to 190°C (375°F). • Peel, halve, and dice the avocados. Place the avocados on a heatproof plate and season with salt. Cover with the avocado oil. Just before plating, place in the oven for 3 minutes.
Assembly	Alfalfa flowers	• To serve, place the avocados on a plate, cover with tamarillo sauce, and top with the algae crunch, beet powder, and alfalfa flowers.

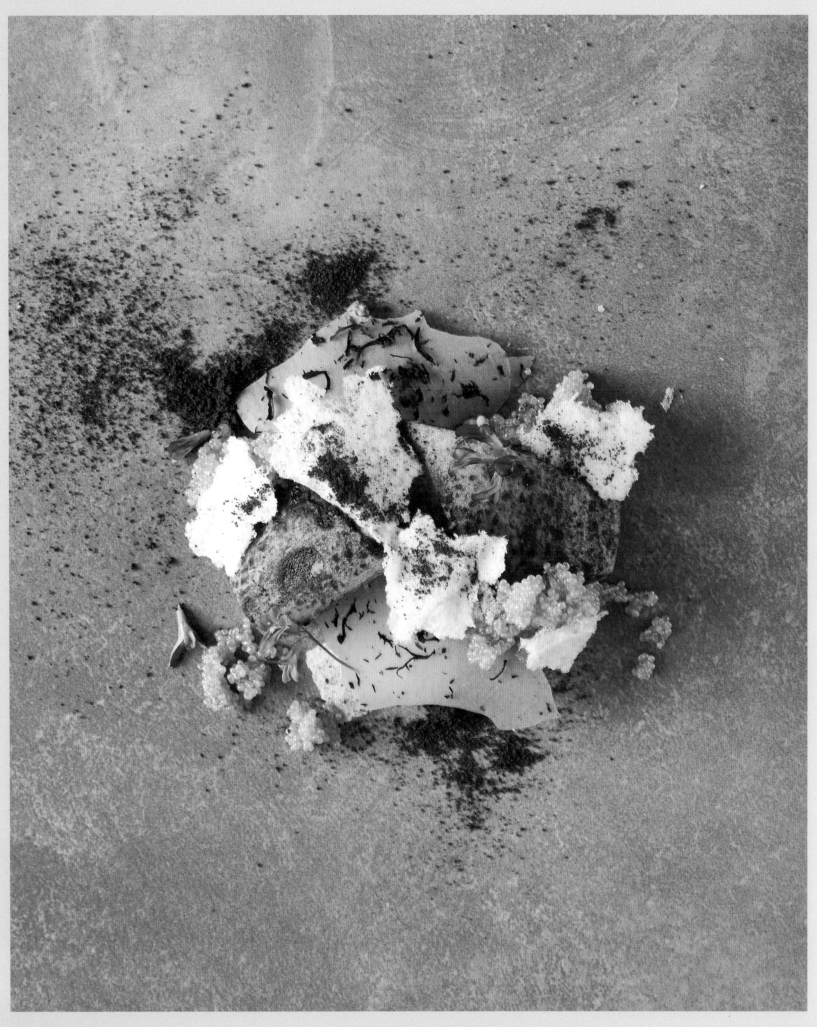

Bajo Andino

Amarillo de tubérculos

YELLOW TUBERS

The first time I tried *arracacha* was in Colombia—and then later in Ecuador. On both occasions, a stew made with chunks of this tuber resulted in a warm and comforting preparation. Here, *arracacha* is finely and carefully laminated, and then *llama charqui* (dehydrated llama meat) is added to incorporate additional salt and flavor. As in other recipes, there is no central ingredient; instead, all the elements play an equally important part. The delicacy of each ingredient, and how it meshes with the other ingredients, dictates how much of each we will use. For example, we use a technique where we pour hot oil over fresh, native herbs that were collected in these valleys to help capture the wild flavors of the soil. It is a reliable way to extract aromas from these valley herbs just before serving.

Serves 6

Tamarillo & Llama Charqui Broth	Dry callampa mushrooms, 300 g Llama charqui, 200 g Dried *tamarillo*, 150 g Avocado leaf, 1 Flaxseeds, 100 g	• In a pot, bring 2 L water to a boil, remove from the heat, and add the dry mushrooms, llama charqui, *tamarillo*, and avocado leaf. Remove from heat, cover, and let the broth infuse and let cool at room temperature. • Meanwhile, soak the flaxseeds in water for 30 minutes; drain to obtain the gel. Set aside until ready to serve.
Herb-Infused Oil	*Huacatay*, 50 g *Chincho*, 10 g *Paico*, 15 g *Culén*, 10 g Avocado oil, 40 ml	• Right before serving, set up a stainless-steel tray at a 30° angle to the work surface. Arrange the *huacatay*, *chincho*, *paico*, and *culén* at the top of the tray. Heat the avocado oil to 160°C (320°F) and pour the hot oil over the herbs. Reserve the oil for plating.
Assembly	*Arracacha*, 1 kg	• When ready to serve, warm the broth in a pot over medium heat until hot. Stir in the reserved flax gel, and, using a spiralizer, make "noodles" with the raw *arrachacha*, and cook them for 10 minutes in the broth. • Divide the *arracacha* noodles among 4 warm bowls and add the hot broth, topping with the herb-infused oil.

Hojas de valle andino

LEAVES OF THE ANDEAN VALLEY

The *chamburu* is known as the mountain papaya. Part of the *Caricaceae* family—small trees with a lineage that traces back millions of years—it grows in the highlands of the region. At this level we also find the greatest variety of herbs and lots of flowers. Unlike the barren lower reaches, the region is green and full of vegetation, color, and life. The climate is mild; there are meandering rivers filled with sounds of birds and insects. Everything is expressive.

Serves 4

Chia seeds, 30 g
Chamburú fruit, 600 g, peeled
Cow´s milk curd, 120 g
Huacatay leaves, 8
Huamanripa leaves, 8
Garlic flowers, 8
Calendula petals, 8
Chincho leaves, 8
Lemon verbena leaves, 8
Retama petals, 8
Cilantro (coriander) flowers, 8
Quinoa leaves, 8
Red oxalis flowers, 8
Paico leaves, 8
Muña leaves, 8
Basil flowers, 8
Malva flowers, 8
Hierba buena leaves, 8
Chia seed oil, 20 ml
Cactus Gel (page 74), 5 g

- Line a 43 x 31 cm (17 x 12-inch) dehydrator tray with a silicone mat.
- Combine the chia seeds with 1 L water and let rest for 10 minutes until the seeds swell. Spread the mixture on the lined tray and dehydrate at 60°C (140°F) for 2 hours or until dry.
- Meanwhile, place the *chamburú* pulp in a blender and blend until smooth. Pass the purée through a fine-mesh sieve, cover, and refrigerate until plating.
- When the chia seed purée is completely dry, break it in a mortar and pestle, and combine with the milk curd and the *chamburú* purée.
- To serve, place a spoon of *chamburú* and milk curd purée in each bowl. Evenly divide the leaves, herbs, and flowers among the bowls. Spray with chia seed oil and top with cactus gel.

Color de airampo

AIRAMPO DYE

Airampo is a variety of *opuntia* (*Opuntia soehrensii*), a small fruit with a fuchsia color that's similar to *tuna* (prickly pear). Its natural habitat is in the Andean foothills, between 800 and 2,800 meters (2,600 and 5,900 feet) above sea level, and the plant consists of a cactus between 1 and 1.5 meters (3 and 5 feet) in height. Like other cacti we have seen on our roads, it is planted to act more as a fence to delineate plots of farmland than for its fruit.

We have two ways to use and preserve airampo. For the first, we remove the pulp and freeze it until needed. The second way is to dehydrate the fruit and conserve the seeds—we then use them to create a vibrant fuchsia dye to color drinks and *mazamorras*, or porridges. The natural dye has also been used in textiles, while infusions of dehydrated seeds are used for their medicinal properties in some communities. We further take advantage of the pulp's acidity and brightness to cure fish, turning it a bright fuchsia color.

Makes 100 g

Airampo fruit, 5 kg

- Remove and seed the pulp from the *airampo* fruit. Pass through a fine-mesh sieve into a bowl. Cover and refrigerate for up to 5 days.

Lúcuma, cactus y retama

LÚCUMA, CACTUS & RETAMA

Cultivated since pre-Columbian times, *lúcuma* is one of our most emblematic fruits. It's yolk-like yellow-orange pulp has a flavor reminiscent of pumpkin and maple, making it a favorite for ice creams and other Peruvian sweets. We've found the flavor naturally balances well with the colorful flowers and herbs that we collect in the fertile valleys around it, like intense yellow *retama* blossoms, *huacatay* leaves, and chamomile flowers.

Serves 6

Lúcuma fruit, 4, peeled
Milk, 500 ml
Egg yolks, 6
Grated panela, 150 g
Hercampuri leaves, 300 g
Stevia Crystals (page 238), 20 g
Cactus Gel (page 74), 300 g
Retama blossoms, 10
Lemon verbena leaves, 10
Huacatay leaves, 10
Chamomile flowers, 10
Carnations petals, 10
Marigolds flowers, 10

- Measure out 50 g of the *lúcuma* pulp and set aside. Transfer the remainder to a blender, add the milk, and blend to a purée. Transfer the purée to a saucepan and bring to a boil.
- Meanwhile, in a bowl, whisk together the egg yolks and panela.
- Stir some of the hot purée into the egg mixture to temper the eggs. Then add the egg mixture to the pan and cook, stirring constantly, over low heat for 10 minutes, until thickened. Strain the mixture through a fine-mesh sieve, let it cool down, and transfer to a pastry bag. Refrigerate until ready to serve.
- Using a mortar and pestle, crush the *hercampuri* leaves with the Stevia crystals.
- To serve, plate the *lúcuma* mixture with the cactus gel. Top with the retama blossoms, *hercampuri*–stevia mixture, lemon verbena, *huacatay*, chamomile, carnation petals, and marigolds.

3,600 m · 11,811 ft

A
N
D
E

As we walk up the mountain to look for herbs from the village of Chahuay, it appears it might rain. The clouds overhead are thick and gray. Francisco Quico Mamani begins blowing into the air. He huffs three times and then puffs three times to his right. Then he does the same to his left. He says it will help the rain stay away for a little while. I don't know if he actually believes his huffing and puffing will stop the rain. Sometimes he says he is full of superpowers—and I generally trust him. I have to respect that his spiritual knowledge has value.

To understand Andean cosmovision, I accept that Francisco's way of looking at the world may not always correlate with mine. The human history of the Andes is considerably different than that of the coast. The hostile geography favors a close relationship with nature, one where reality is based on the cyclical rhythm of the universe. When Francisco's wife, Trinidad, boils potatoes, she is careful not to dump the water on the ground. "The earth needs to stay calm," she says. It's part of a larger belief: When nature is disturbed, it can create chaos, a misbalance. Plants and nature can help restore order.

We drove south that morning for several hours on a road that connects Cuzco to the *altiplano* and Lake Titicaca, to reach Chahuay, where we find Francisco and Trinidad, who have become our primary links to the ancestral knowledge of the *Quechua* people. Even in the face of encroaching technology they have managed to maintain traditions that date back centuries. We have been working with them since we had our restaurant, Senzo, in Cuzco and continue to develop a stronger relationship with them.

The clouds seem to lift as we climb higher, parting to show us a bright blue sky. Lately, the weather has been acting strange here—and all over Peru. In Lima, the temperature has been cooler than normal for this time of year. Here, the rainy season would typically have already begun and the mountains would have turned green, but this year, it's late and the mountains are still brown.

We follow a small stream for several hundred meters and Francisco points out that there is *cushuro*, a spherical bacteria, growing within. Normally we find *cushuro* in stagnant water on lakeshores, where you can scoop it by the bucket. Here it is in small patches, clinging to rocks, and the shape is more blob-like. We collect some in a glass jar to bring back to Lima to study it more.

We pass ruins of old adobe houses where *queuña* trees grow out of the trapezoid-shaped windows that are customary in Incan architecture. The houses are hundreds of years old, yet Francisco tells stories about them as if they were still being used. He speaks of Túpac Amaru II, the Inca revolutionary who launched a rebellion against Spanish rule. Francisco marches along the ridge, describing specific weapons the rebels carried, as if they were there yesterday. In his worldview, time and space occur within an equilibrium.

Further up the mountain are where the herbs are. I once asked Francisco and Trinidad why they don't just plant them near their house and they laughed. It's dirty there. That's where they live, where the dogs and cats are. Up the mountain it is clean and pure. The closer you are to the apex, the mountaintop, the more sacred the earth is.

Francisco and Trini don't cook with herbs and find it odd that I do. They all have medicinal uses, so they typically use the herbs in infusions. As we walk they point out *Inca muña*, a wild variety of what is sometimes called Andean mint, which they use to treat respiratory problems. There is *chiri chiri*, a large root, used for healing bruises, and the aromatic *pampa anis* for muscle spasms. They know everything about every herb that grows here; these herbs have been used by generation upon generation. Every few steps they describe something I've never heard of. In their heads is a database of hundreds, maybe more, of plants. They know how factors such as the temperature, light, and soil affect the size, shape, and intensity of the medicinal properties of each.

When we descend to their house, we begin preparing a *huatia*, a dome-shaped earthen oven made of mud bricks and stones. The oven has two holes: a large one in the front where the kindling is put—and another in the back to release some of the smoke. It only takes about ten minutes to make the oven, then maybe another hour or so to get it to the right temperature, which varies by the dryness of the soil, wind, and humidity. Trini can just look at the oven and know when it is ready. She keeps adding fava bean leaves and eucalyptus and queuña branches until the bricks become charred and black. When the potatoes are added, the oven, already on the verge of collapse, gets knocked apart. The stones get pulled out by hand and the mud bricks get chopped apart with a pickaxe until there is just a mound of hot, tightly packed dirt and potatoes. The tubers are returned to the earth they came from and then are eaten, uniting man with *pachamama*, mother earth.

This feast is usually prepared on the mountain, during a harvest, for everyone who has been working steadily in the cold and wind at this dizzying height. The potatoes, *ocas*, and *mashuas* are gathered on a colorful *manta* and brought to the oven and cooked inside. It's a simple, nourishing meal. Aside from these potatoes, someone might bring fresh cheese and *uchucuta*, a chile sauce, but little else. We remove the tubers and wipe off the dirt. We return them to the *manta*. As we eat, we remove the skins and toss them in a pile, to be reused as compost and put back into the soil. Suddenly, it begins to rain.

Ocas y ollucos en Maras

OCAS & OLLUCOS IN MARAS

The Salineras de Maras dramatically drape the steep slopes of Qaqawiñay mountain, 3,380 meters (11,090 feet) above sea level outside of Cuzco. Each of the small salt ponds has a deed that has been passed down from family to family, much like the deed of a house, for generations, since well before the Inca Empire ever came to be. The pale pink salt has become a gourmet product in recent years, appearing on restaurant menus and in upscale food shops.

On the road to the salt ponds we often pass plots of *oca* in the neighboring community of Maras. Oca (*Oxalis tuberosa*) is one of the emblematic crops of this altitude, second only to the potato in agricultural importance. The hardy, highly nutritious root vegetable can be planted in the harshest climates at Peru's highest elevations. They are usually sprouting leaves or flowers, which we collect up until the point of harvest, an exciting activity that we try to bring much of the team from Central to experience. The *oca* here tastes sweet and slightly spicy with a hint of nuts. This recipe visualizes Maras as we have seen it: the search for salt and the harvesting of *oca*.

Serves 8

Maras salt, 1 kg
Chaco clay, 200 g
Egg whites, 250 g
Ocas, 150 g
Ollucos, 150 g

- Preheat the oven to 250°C (482°F).
- In a bowl, combine the salt and *chaco* clay with the egg whites. Spread half the mixture to a 2.5 cm (1-inch) thickness on a 43 x 31 cm (17 x 12-inch) rimmed baking sheet. Place the *ocas* and *ollucos* on top and cover with the remainder of the egg white mixture. Bake for exactly 35 minutes.
- Remove from the oven and gently break the salt crust with a mallet. Serve the *ocas* and *ollucos* immediately.

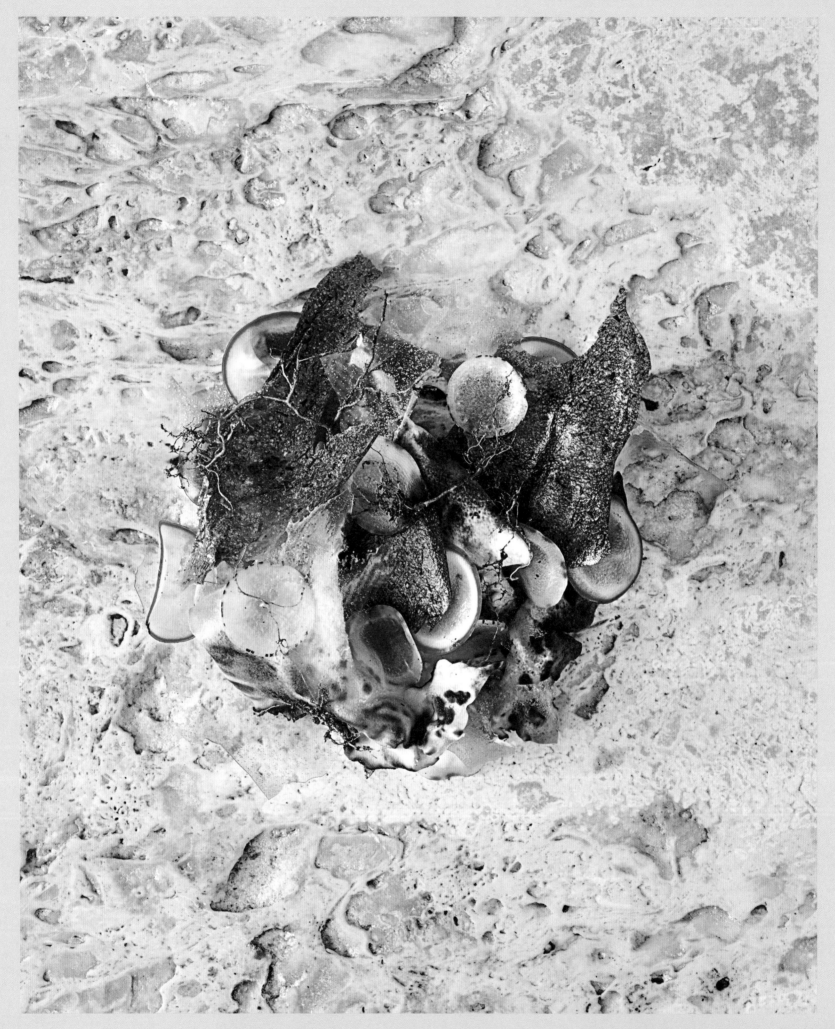

Ande

Tallos extremos

EXTREME STEMS

This dish captures the nature, colors, smells, and textures of the *serranía esteparia*, the mountainous steppe—an ecoregion where tubers, such as *ocas* and *ollucos*, coexist with different leaves and herbs that also favor the steppe's extreme altitude. While the tubers grow at other altitudes, here in their natural habitat, they are most expressive of their terroir. We can make this dish year round, as the ingredients can be found throughout the seasons and at slightly lower elevations, grown on small family farms.

Serves 8

Oca Dough & Mashua Skin	*Ocas*, 2 kg Maras salt, 1 kg *Chaco* clay, 200 g Egg whites, 250 g Potato starch, 200 g Egg yolks, 6 *Mashua* leaves, 400 g	• Follow the directions in Ocas in Maras (page 103) for baking the *ocas* in a salt crust, using the Maras salt, *chaco* clay, and egg whites. Remove the salt from the baked *ocas* with a wet kitchen towel. Set aside half of the *ocas* for the *oca* skin. • In a blender, combine the remaining hot *ocas* with the potato starch and egg yolks and process on high speed for 5 minutes until well combined. With your hands, shape the dough into small disks slightly larger than 1 cm (1/2 inch) in diameter. Divide in half and refrigerate, covered, until ready to plate. • Make the *oca* skin: Line 2 (43 x 31 cm/17 x 12–inch) dehydrator trays with silicone mats. Using a potato masher, make a purée with the reserved baked *ocas*. Pass through a fine-mesh sieve and spread half of the purée on a lined tray. • Make the *mashua* skin: Juice the *mashua* leaves, and combine juice with the remainder of the purée. Spread the *mashua* purée on another lined tray. Transfer the trays to a dehydrator and dehydrate the purées at 45°C (113°F) for 2 hours or until dry.
Olluco Sauce	Corn oil, 15 ml Onion, 500 g, julienned *Ollucos*, 50 pieces Salt	• In a skillet, warm the oil over medium heat. Add the onions and cook, stirring from time to time, until caramelized, about 10 minutes. Set aside 4 of the *olluco* pieces and add the remainder to the onions. Cook without stirring, uncovered, for 20 minutes, or until soft. Add 400 ml water and cook for 20 minutes to reduce by half; the mixture will become uniform. Pass through a fine chinois and season with salt.
Assembly	Corn oil, 5 ml Andean butter, 100 g	• When ready to serve, in a hot pan over medium heat the oil and the butter and sauté the *oca* discs for 1 minute until golden brown. • Thinly slice the reserved *ollucos*, for the final plating. • Place the cooked *olluco* discs on the dish, cover with the *olluco* sauce, and top with the *oca* dough and mashua skins, and reserved sliced *ollucos*.

Papeles de queñual

QUEÑUAL PAPER

The previous recipes in this chapter utilize *ocas*, *ollucos*, potatoes, and other tubers from this part of the Andes. All these crops share the soil at this elevation with the cultivation of quinoa and the *queñual*, an endemic species of tree that forms part of the traditional landscape. It's often found in the forests of protected areas, home to numerous herbs, many of which have yet to be studied. Walking through these forests is surreal: The fragile, paper-thin layers of bark peel off of the *queñual*, moving in the wind, changing the focus of your eyes. It is a tree that serves multiple purposes where it grows. It regulates the climate, stores large amounts of water, feeds springs, and prevents soil erosion. For these reasons, in places where it is found, you find many other wild species of plants cohabit the same terrain. There are more than enough reasons to keep *queñuals* from being cut down, however, over the past few centuries, faster growing eucalyptus trees have gradually replaced them.

At Central, we make a light infusion using only the bark of the *queñual* that falls to the forest floor. In many Andean communities this bark is considered to have medicinal properties, though for our purposes we use it to add an earthy aroma to the dish, to bring a sense of place and awareness of the ecosystem that the *queñual* represents.

Serves 4

Queñual bark, 100 g
Ocas, 300 g
Red oxalis leaves, 200 g
Cilantro (coriander) flowers
Quinoa leaves
Kiwicha leaves

- In a saucepan, combine 500 ml water and the *queñual* bark and bring to a boil over high heat. Remove from the heat, cover, and let steep for 10 minutes. Strain the infusion and keep the bark for garnish.
- Meanwhile, in another saucepan, combine the *ocas* with water to cover and cook over medium heat for 40 minutes. Drain and pass the *ocas* through a fine-mesh sieve; let the *ocas* cool. In a blender, combine the *ocas* with the red oxalis and purée until smooth. Pass the purée through a fine-mesh sieve into a bowl, cover, and refrigerate until cold.
- Add the *queñual* infusion using a dropper, 6 drops at a time. Divide among 4 crystal glasses. Garnish each glass with the *queñual* bark, cilantro flowers, and quinoa and *kiwicha* leaves.

Cerdo en mashuas

PORK IN MASHUAS

On the way up, deeper into the mountains, we usually pass through wild landscapes full of *yuyos*, the flowering weeds of the *pampas*. Pigs are a part of the journey too, seen around the communities and farms. They are fed the *pampas* roots, which have a strong flavor of horseradish. The *mashuas*, a high-yielding, disease-resistant tuber, thrive here too, competing with weeds for nutrients. After harvest, *mashuas* are left in the sun for four or five days, letting the starches convert to sugar, resulting in a sweeter flavor. We play on this sweetness with the flowers of *frutilla*, a local strawberry that also grows here. We use the nectar to give another dimension to the sauce, which combines all the components of the recipe and unites the dish.

Serves 4

Yellow *mashua*, 300 g
Purple *mashua*, 300 g
Pork spare ribs, 700 g
Frutilla flower nectar, 50 ml
Tarwi, 120 g
Olive oil, 20 ml
Pampa yuyo branches, 1 bunch

- In a saucepan, bring 2 L of water to a boil over high heat. Add the yellow and purple *mashuas* and cook, uncovered, for 14 minutes, until soft but firm. Drain the *mashuas*, reserving the cooking water. Peel the *mashuas* and reserve the skin. Place the skin on a dehydrator tray and dehydrate at 45°C (113°F) for 8 hours until dry.
- In a pot, combine the pork with the reserved *mashua* cooking water, cover, and cook over low heat for 7 hours, or until the meat is tender. Remove from the heat. Reserving the broth, drain and set the meat aside.
- Add the *frutilla* nectar to the broth and weigh the mixture. Return the mixture to a saucepan and cook over low heat until the liquid is reduced to one-third of its liquid weight. Remove from the heat and set aside.
- In a saucepan, bring to boil 1 L of water to a boil over high heat. Add the *tarwi*, reduce the heat to low and cook, uncovered, for 4 hours until soft. Transfer to a blender and purée with the olive oil until smooth. Pass through a fine-mesh sieve to obtain a completely smooth paste.
- To serve, remove the pork from the ribs (discard the bones). Spread the the *frutilla* flower reduction over the meat and place it over the *tarwi* paste. Top with the *pampa yuyo* branches and the *mashua* skin, and serve.

Ande

Dulce mashua

SWEET MASHUA

We started to work with *mashua* around Central's second year, which was an oversight on our part, because it is as much a part of our area as it is of the Andes. It took us another year to begin to understand it as we began to see vital distinctions among its different parts while on our exploration trips with Mater. There were the thickened stems, branches, and the first leaves that sprouted from the plant, which could be eaten. We started to see the beauty of the plant's extremities: the tuber's lines, colors, and different flavors. In its raw state, it is like an anise-flavored radish—slightly spicy and sweet. After being harvested, it spends a few days on the ground taking in the sun, sweetened by the same earth it was grown in.

Serves 4

Purple *mashua*, 420 g
Yellow *mashua*, 420 g
Yacón Crystals (see page 239), 300 g
Yacón molasses, 30 ml
Butter, 200 g
Nasturtium flowers, 4
Paico leaves, 8
Cedrón leaves, 8

- Preheat the oven to 200°C (392°F). Arrange 120 g (about 2) of purple *mashua* on a rimmed baking sheet, toss with 100 g of the *yacón* crystals, and bake for 2 hours ,or until the *mashua* is cooked through and caramelized. Remove from the oven and set aside. Keep the oven on, but reduce the temperature to 110°C (230°F).
- Cut 120 g of the yellow *mashua* into halves and arrange on a rimmed baking sheet. Toss with 100 g of the *yacón* crystals and bake for 15 minutes, or until the *mashua* is cooked through and caramelized. Remove from the oven and set aside. Keep the oven on.
- Combine the remaining 300 g of purple *mashua* with the *yacón* molasses and 100 g of butter, put on a baking sheet and bake for 2 hours, or until caramelized. Using a masher, mash the cooked purple *mashua* into a fine purée, transfer to round molds, and refrigerate until firm.
- In a pot, combine the remaining 300 g of the yellow *mashua* with enough water to cover, bring to a boil over high heat, and cook until soft. Remove from the heat, cool, and peel. Discard the skins and blend the boiled *mashua* with the remaining 100 g of butter and 100 g of *yacón* crystals. Pass through a sieve and reserve hot for the plating.
- Cut the nasturtium flowers into fine julienne.
- To serve, place the *mashuas* (purple and yellow) on a green stone with the round shape of purple *mashua*. Place the yellow hot *mashua* purée alongside and cover with the nasturtium julienne. Top with the *paico* and *cedrón* leaves between the *mashuas*.

Corazón

HEART

While our Andean landscape is painted with grazing cattle, we're not big beef eaters, even in this part of the Andes—nor, for that matter, in the lowlands of the Amazon. Dairy generates more curiosity in our kitchens than meat does. However, beef heart is symbolic in Peru and has a diverse set of uses, like the *anticuchos* we eat at our family meals at the restaurant, marinated and grilled on skewers, or used in stews.

In the three or four times a beef preparation appears on the menu each year, we try to include the heart, as a symbol of our Peruvian identity. Here, the heart complements the environment where we find the cow, grazing on the herbs and grasses at this altitude. This entire process of cleaning, marinating, and drying the heart on the day of the slaughter is what we have tried to translate to the plate. In this case, an assortment of herbs are mixed into the raw heart to balance the slightly spicy *ají panca* sauce and the Maras salt, both of which help to dry and cure the meat until it reaches the texture we want.

This recipe is for a seasoning. We add a pinch of grated heart to our pseudocereals dish, for example.

Makes about 80 g

Maras salt, 2 kg
Ají panca, 300 g
Chicha de jora, 50 ml
Chincho, 10 g
Huamanripa, 10 g
Grasses from the altitude, 10 g, chopped
Beef heart, 1

- In a bowl, mix together the salt, *ají panca*, *chicha de jora*, *chincho*, *huamanripa*, and grasses to make a thick paste.
- Remove half of the fat from the heart and discard. Rub the heart with the paste and refrigerate for 5 hours. Using a clean cloth, wipe the cure off of the heart.
- Ideally, hang the heart in a cool, dark spot at 10°C (50°F) for about 19 hours in a well-ventilated room—such as a windowed room that's in a particularly windy spot. This process works best if done in the mountains, at this specific altitude, in a dark room with a window facilitating the entrance of the wind. We've learned this from doing this process for over 3 years. You can also fashion a hook in your refrigerator and hang the heart there. We serve the heart grated like jerky; it has a firmer and drier consistency than prosciutto.

4,200 m · 13,780 ft

ALTURA EXTREMA

We set out in complete darkness. By the time the sun rises, we are halfway up the Cordillera Negra and it zigzags in such a way that we can easily distinguish between the white and black ridges of the mountains. We pass the village of Recuay and beneath Cerro Huancapetí, a dramatic landscape of steep cliffs and narrow valleys where very little grows.

We take out coca leaves as soon as we get 2,000 meters (6,560 feet) above sea level. We have to—for the energy. We take a chunk of *llipta*, which is quinoa or *kañiwa* ash that has been formed into a sort of resin, almost like hashish, and wrap it with fresh coca leaves. Then we put it in our mouths to chew, keeping it right inside our cheeks.

At this altitude, you feel an influx of emotions. The lack of oxygen makes it hard to breathe; your head becomes heavy, dizzy; every movement is a struggle. The pressure of the altitude numbs the body—it's just you, exposed and unprotected, and the natural world. Yet there is also a sense of calm here. There is this paradox: You are on top of all of this biodiversity; below are tens of thousands of species of plants and animals—many of them found only there—but here it seems as if there is nothing around you. Even with a strong wind, there is nothing here to make a sound, not even living creatures. The llamas and alpacas don't come up this high. There are no green vegetation or trees from the high Amazonian landscapes. We have left the colorful flowers of the valleys behind us. There are patches of *ichu*—long grasses—but little else. You are alone. There are just the *apus*, the peaks of the Andes, there to protect you. *Pachamama*—mother earth—is here with you. You can feel your own presence more clearly here than at lower altitudes.

The sun is shining brightly by the time we arrive in Ajia. From the plaza we walk to the house of farmer Adrián Fernandez Brito. His daughter, Maria Luisa, greets us, smiling, and invites us into their home, a typical house made of mud bricks, painted pink, with a red clay tile roof. We walk down a hallway that exits into an interior garden. One corner is dedicated to a small pen for the *cuy*, or guinea pigs, while larger animals like chickens and goats fill a larger space. Steam from the heat of bacterial decomposition rises off a compost bin made of enormous wooden crates—filled with fodder, crop residues, the remains of guinea pigs, and worms—covered in natural fibers and straw.

The kitchen in the back is dark with a low-ceiling overhead. There's a large table, a wood-burning stove, iron and clay pots, and some twine from which hang hulking legs of pork cured with spices and salt. There are also animal skins, a plate with thin strips of meat, and lake fish that has been cured and dried.

Out of a pot Brito ladles a typical country breakfast to start the day: *caldo de carnero*, a mutton soup. It's a thin mixture with *muña* and chives, along with fibrous chunks of meat, a touch of salt, and some herbs we can't identify. Maria Luisa says that it is common to make a special combination of herbs and roots like *huamanpinta*, *cedroncillo*, and *matico*, to name a few. In white tin cups we are given a muña infusion, which helps with the dizzying altitude. Maria Luisa serves us warmly, with an incredible affection that you rarely see in a big city.

Afterwards, Brito shows us more of his garden. There are *ocas*, aromatic herbs, and vines of *tumbo*. Then there's a *saúco* shrub, a type of native elderberry. Beneath a *fitotoldo*, a small greenhouse, are tomatoes, *ajíes*, and zucchini—ingredients we're accustomed to on the coast. At this altitude, they almost seem out of place. We lean against a wall and take in the fresh air and morning sun.

This is a part of Peru where we have only scratched the surface in terms of what is here. We are the first group of cooks trying to bring ingredients from this altitude. These ingredients have never seen a formal kitchen and some are contained within a single valley. Much is unknown. Not just the plants, but how humans have managed to survive in such a harsh terrain.

For a chef, this landscape presents many challenges. Aside from the physical challenges of the altitude, the sources of inspiration are not as evident as in places like the jungle, where every tree can be an entire ecosystem. In these extreme conditions—the frigid wind, lack of oxygen, and intensity of the sun—many of the most incredible plants are forced to grow unseen. You have to look deeper, to dig beneath the earth for tubers, to pick the *ichu* and grab the *mashuas* and *ocas*. The roots are submerged in the soil. While this landscape may appear unwelcoming, it must also be very rich to be able to develop these unique ingredients that concentrate so much flavor.

Amid this harsh landscape, with all of its difficulties, this humble farmer plods on, working his crops as if he were anywhere else. As we have seen in Cuzco many times before, Brito is working the land at different altitudes. It allows him to cultivate more varieties of crops in places with varying levels of humidity or amounts of minerals in the soil. His commitment to preserving the region's biodiversity is amazing.

Brito leads us to one field, a half hectare (1 acre) of sloping terrain where he recently planted different varieties of native tubers. Some of the ocas and mashuas have already begun flowering. There are *purush* flowers, *tarwi*, strawberries, and an amazing variety of wild herbs, as diverse as anywhere we've seen in the region. Pickaxe in hand, he walks ahead, with a step much lighter than ours. At nearly seventy-years-old, Brito has lived all of his life in Ajia. Despite the recent passing of his wife, he is content with his life in the field. Some of his children work with him, while one is a teacher who works lower down the mountain. His granddaughter, Lidsay, a biology student at San Marcos University in Lima, brings us transparent buckets filled with Brito's crops, which are tightly packed in woven fiber bags.

Brito has worked the land as long as he can remember. The parents and grandparents of farmers in the area say he knows all the fields—down below, beside the river, the place above the eucalyptus, and on the slopes looking down on the valley—and "how they behave," as if the fields were living, breathing creatures. He has seen the land change with the passage of time—not just season after season, but decade after decade. It has become an indelible part of him. There is so much we can learn.

He takes us to a stream where he has buried potatoes in a hole layered with stones and *ichu* to make *tocosh*, a centuries-old process of potato fermentation. They are the firm Canchan potatoes, neutral in flavor and not too bitter, though he sometimes uses ocas, mashuas, and other varieties of tubers, or even maize. He digs through the mud and grasses, now intertwined with the potatoes, to show us the transformation. The small potatoes have become blackened after having undergone a process of bacterial fermentation and putrefaction for the past month. The smell is unbearable. There's nothing I've ever smelled in my life that is so strong.

Seeing this incredible process of converting native potatoes into this product that is very rooted to the culture, we realize that it must be a part of our menu. It has to be valued and recognized. It doesn't matter if the smell or flavor causes a bit of discomfort. It's a reminder of how estranged we are from some of our own ingredients, and that's exactly what we should change.

Tocosh

We gather our *tocosh* (fermented potatoes) from Aija, a village near Huaraz, the capital of the Ancash region at 3,800 meters (12,000 feet). We visit from time to time to see how the process is going, then when the *tocosh* is ready, we bring it to Central.

Makes 5 kf

Dried *ichu*, 2 kg
Canchan potatoes, 5 kg
Special equipment: 1 to 3 kg stones,
   enough to cover the potatoes

- On the edge of a stream or river, dig a small hole about 1 m (3 feet) in diameter and about 60 cm (2 feet) deep.
- Build a "nest" with half the *ichu* at the bottom of the hole and place the potatoes inside the nest. Cover with the remaining *ichu*. Place the stones on top, allowing the current to flow through the stones during the fermentation process. Leave the potatoes for 30 days and up to 45 days. Throughout this period, you must constantly check on the potatoes in case they are ready before the month is out. The potatoes should be a dark color and will have an intense aroma.
- Place the potatoes in a dry shaded area and allow the water to drain. The *tocosh* is now ready to be consumed. It is traditionally stored in fiber bags, though can also be sun-dried and ground into a powder.

Fermentación en los Andes

FERMENTATION IN THE ANDES

Tocosh can be hard for some to understand. It's a process of potato preservation by fermentation and dehydration that originated in the central Andes, from Huanuco to Huaraz, sometime during the Chavín era (900 BC to 200 BC), which ended more than 2,000 years ago. The strong flavor and aroma can frighten and confuse some. "Why degrade a perfect tuber for something so rancid?" someone might ask. Different varieties, at different prices, are sold across Peruvian markets. They can come peeled or unpeeled and are sorted by how many days the potatoes have been fermented. *Tocosh* is used in stews or to make mazamorra de *tocosh*, a porridge that locals prepare by boiling *tocosh* with water, sugar, cinnamon, and cloves. Fermentation can beget penicillin, and *tocosh* has been said to be a cure for various bacterial infections, along with stomach ulcers, gastritis, digestion, and respiratory illnesses, as well as altitude sickness. Around the region, families have it on their table like we would have bread.

When we get *tocosh* in the kitchen at Central, everyone stops what they are doing. You can't ignore the smell—it's like a really potent cheese. I'm not sure if I should laugh or feel badly for the person who must peel the potatoes. I know, personally, as does Pía, that every time you peel off *tocosh* skin, the aroma lingers on your fingers for a few days. Still, I have always felt it was worth the effort to find ways to serve *tocosh* at Central. It's a challenge we continue to work on. Often, we use it as a thickener, though in this recipe we dehydrate the skin and then deep-fry it. It winds up looking like a *chicharrón* and we serve it as a part of the bread course. It's a way to retain some of the health benefits and nutrients of *tocosh* without bringing the smell into the dining room.

Serves 12

Tocosh (page 126), 600 g
Pork fat, 500 g
Maras salt, 2 g

- Very carefully, peel the *tocosh*, reserving the skins (save the rest of the potatoes for another use). Place the skins on a dehydrator tray, season with salt, and dehydrate at 55°C (131°F) for about 6 hours, or until they are completely dried.
- In a heavy saucepan, heat the fat to 180°C (356°F) over medium heat. Carefully slide the dehydrated skins into the fat and deep-fry about 1 minute, or until golden brown. Transfer the fried skins to a plate lined with paper towels to absorb the extra oil.

Altura Extrema

Choclos andinos

ANDEAN CORN

Varieties of maize are found across many microclimates in Peru, though we encountered this simple preparation while searching for the maize that grows in the high Andes. At these heights corn is ground in a mortar to a coarse powder, then dried and stored in huts. These powders are ideal for storage, even in places where the temperature isn't controlled. Andean communities have survived for centuries in these extreme environments by doing just this. While participating in a *huatia*, where tubers are cooked in an earthen oven made of mud bricks during a harvest, these dense maize blocks are often found on the side, cooked in the same soil. They're compact yet heavy, and in a single bite you can get a sense of the earth that the maize is coming from—the soul of the maize. This was our discovery—or rather rediscovery—of a recipe that is basic in many communities. We haven't found a way to achieve the same flavors and aromas in Central—the ones that we encounter during a *huatia*. We're simply not in the moment or the place, nor do we have the outdoor space to prepare a proper *huatia*. But we come pretty close.

Makes 30 pieces

Milk, 1.2 L
Chuncho corn, 100 g, very finely ground
Salt, 25 g
Andean butter, 300 g
Corn flour, 600 g
Eggs, 8, separated
Chullpi corn, 120 g, crushed

- In a saucepan, bring the milk to a boil over medium heat. Add the corn powder and salt and mix well. Stir in the butter and corn flour until incorporated, then remove from the heat. Add the egg yolks, one at a time, waiting to add the next one until each yolk is fully incorporated.
- In a clean bowl, whip the egg whites until stiff peaks form. Gently fold the corn mixture into the egg whites.
- Transfer the batter to a container and, using an offset spatula, smooth out the top. Refrigerate the batter for 2 hours.
- Preheat the oven to 180°C (356°F).
- Cut the batter into 6 irregular blocks, dip each block in the Chullpi corn to coat on all sides, and then cut each block into 25 g (about 1-ounce) pieces. Knead each piece into a ball, and using a firm, flat surface, press each ball into a disk and set each one in a tray with round molds about 4 cm (1½-inches) in diameter.
- Bake the disks for 22 minutes, or until golden brown. Finish with a torch.

Tin Tin

TIN TIN

This idea is formulated around a group of Andean herbs that are typically sold and bundled together in markets and are used for medicinal purposes. Conveniently, all four—*muña, huacatay, paico,* and *chincho*—grow on our roof garden. The signature ingredient is *tin tin (Passiflora pinnatistipula),* a climbing vine with a pink flower and an oblong yellow fruit, which grows in the Andes some 2,500 meters (8,200 feet) above sea level.

Serves 8

Tin tin fruit, 1 kg
Chuño powder, 100 g
Muña, 1 kg
Huacatay leaves, 100 g
Paico, 500 g
Chincho, 200 g
Huacatay flowers, 10

- Scrape the pulp from inside the *tin tins.* Transfer half of the fruit pulp to a blender and purée until smooth. Set the remaining pulp aside.
- Transfer the *tin tin* purée to a saucepot, stir in the *chuño* powder, and cook over low heat until you have a gel. Divide the mixture in half.
- In a juicer, juice the *muña, huacatay* leaves, *paico,* and *chincho* to extract the chlorophyll. Stir the chlorophyll into half of the *tin tin* mixture.
- Line two dehydrator trays with silicone mats. Spread each of the two *tin tin* mixtures on a lined tray. Dehydrate for 5 hours at 60°C (140°F). Set the dried *tin tin* aside. Break the sheets into pieces.
- To serve, place the remaining *tin tin* mixtures on each of 8 plates and cover with the pieces of dry *tin tin* sheets. Finish with *huacatay* flowers.

Altura Extrema

Alpaca y kiwicha

ALPACA & AMARANTH

One of the most common images of the high Andes is alpaca grazing on fields amid a backdrop of mountain peaks. You'll find countless postcards depicting the scene. This dish returns the alpaca to this landscape, a place of wild herbs and grains.

Serves 4

Alpaca neck, 400 g
Annatto oil, 20 ml
Maras salt
Alpaca milk, 1 L
Kiwicha leaves, 500 g
Kiwicha grains, 100 g
Coffee beans, 20 g

- Remove the fat from the alpaca neck and finely dice. Combine the meat with the fat. Dress with oil and salt to taste.
- Line a dehydrator tray with a silicone mat. Bring the the alpaca milk to a boil and, using an immersion blender, whip the milk for 2 minutes until there is a lot of foam. Spread the milk foam carefully over the lined tray and dehydrate at 70°C (158°F) for 15 hours.
- To extract the clorophyll, pass the *kiwicha* leaves through a juicer.
- In a saucepan with boiling water, cook the *kiwicha* grains for 5 minutes. Drain the *kiwicha*, let cool completely, and mix with the *kiwicha* chlorophyll.
- Grate the coffee beans on top of the plate and place the alpaca neck in the center of the plate. Top with the milk crust and green *kiwicha*.

Altura Extrema

Recolección de cushuro

GATHERING OF CUSHURO

Perhaps the most inclusive and constructive experience for the team is to search for *cushuro*. They are never found as easily as we would like, in high-altitude lagoons or small waterfalls, so we walk slowly, while talking, searching for the right paths. We have had to figure out ways around landslides and ice. Our progress has been halted by heavy rain and fast-moving streams. The criteria for finding *cushuro* and the herbs are not who you know or who goes with you, but rather conveying a sense of balance and harmony with the environment. If we pick too many herbs, we might not find the *cushuro*. If we gather more *cushuro* than we need, the herbs we find might be shriveled. If we are talking to each other and forget to listen to the sounds of the streams or the wind, the path never seems to go where we hope it will. I do not usually pray, nor do many others on the team, but on these days I can ensure you that 90 percent of us will be on our knees.

Serves 8

White quinoa, 300 g
Quinoa leaves, 200 g
Muña leaves, 50 g
Lemon verbena, 50 g
Chincho, 30 g
Paico leaves, 20 g
Quinoa flowers, 6
Red oxalis leaves, 10
Cilantro (coriander) flowers, 6
Stevia leaves, 10
Chaco clay, 100 g
Cushuro, 180 g, peeled
Salt, 2 g
Black quinoa, 100 g
Cabuya molasses, 30 ml
Sacha inchi oil, 20 ml

- To make the quinoa milk, in a blender combine the quinoa with 500 ml of water and blend on high speed until smooth.
- In a saucepan, bring the 600 ml of the quinoa milk to a boil. Blanch half of all the herbs—quinoa leaves, *muña* leaves, lemon verbena, *chincho*, *paico leaves*, quinoa flowers, red oxalis, cilantro flowers, and stevia—for 2 seconds.
- In a blender, purée the burnt quinoa milk with the blanched herbs until smooth. Strain the mixture through a fine-mesh sieve and refrigerate.
- In a blender, process the *chaco* clay until it forms a fine powder. Set aside.
- Blend the burnt herb milk with 100 g of *cushuro* and salt to get thicker milk.
- In a saucepan, combine the black quinoa, 500 ml water, and the *cabuya* molasses, and cook over medium heat for 10 minutes. Line a dehydrator tray with a silicone mat. Drain the black quinoa and spread in the lined tray. Dehydrate at 65°C (149°F) for 2 hours. Then, using a blender, pulverize to a coarse powder.
- To serve, layer the *cushuros* with the thickened herbal milk, and drizzle the *sacha inchi* oil on top. Scatter the herbs over the plate and sprinkle the powder over the dish.

3,900 m · 12,795 ft

A
L
T
I
P
L
A
N
O

ALTIPLANO

There are no winding and steep curves in the *altiplano*, nor colorful green valleys, nor striking mountains. It feels so different to still be in the high Andes without moving in a pattern of ups and downs over the terrain. Here the landscape is flat and the color of straw. It's of golden *ichu* grasses, *totora* reeds, and isolated villages of houses with red clay tile roofs that clash with the blueness of the lake and sky.

In a southerly direction from Puno, we follow a road that skirts the dark blue waters of Lake Titicaca. We pass Chucuito, then Acora, and finally Ilave, driving beyond the village to the community of Chijichaya. We have heard of this Puneña community that for many generations has freeze-dried potatoes in a special way, through a very demanding and meticulous process called *tunta*.

In Chijichaya, after harvest, potatoes are distributed among the peasant farmers of the countryside: The highest quality is for consumption and trade, and the remainder is freeze-dried. Tunta, also called white *chuño* or *moraya*, ensures that for the rest of the year there will be potatoes for soup and hot dishes, where they are rehydrated and flavored with wild herbs. For locals, the intense smell, a matter of habit and even identity, it is not something to be diluted. The comforting taste of cooked chuño with a slice of queso fresco serves as a reminder of home.

The fields surrounding Ilave are used almost exclusively for making tunta, according to Ernesto Chura, an agronomist from Puno who accompanies us. Here in the darkness, on a ground covered with straw, the potatoes are exposed to the frigid temperatures of the altiplano night, which can drop to –10 degrees Celsius (14 degrees Fahrenheit). Just before the sun rises, the potatoes are completely covered with a mesh tarp, preventing the process of oxidization from taking root in daytime temperatures, which can range from 13 to 18 degrees Celsius (55 to 64 degrees Fahrenheit).

We see huge mounds laid out in groups, arranged by their place of origin. A producer approaches us to explain the current state of each. He carefully lifts a corner of the mesh covering of one of the mounds and takes a potato in each hand. He hits them together, making a sound as if he was hitting two stones against one another—they're frozen solid. We smile and touch the potatoes to corroborate how cold and hard they are.

A few minutes further down the road we come to the edge of the Río Ilave. On the banks of the slow-moving river are frozen potatoes that have been soaking for three to four weeks. Rectangular wells, covered with nets, have been built to house these slumbering tubers. After the potatoes are done soaking, they are removed using *wiscañas*, enormous strainers, and rest out of the water overnight. The next day, the peeling starts. This is done by standing on the potatoes while they are covered with *taquiñas* (nets), which causes the skin to peel off with contact.

The peeled potatoes rest on woven grass covers beside the wells they were soaked in. They are exposed to the sunlight for about seven days, spread out to accelerate moisture loss. The homogeneous whiteness of each, determined by the proper management of each step in avoiding oxidation, is a requirement for these producers who expect the highest quality. The more uniform the whiteness, the higher the quality.

We help in the process of picking out those potatoes that are ready. Two people hold each end of a colorful *manta* that can hold about forty kilos. A white dust falls off of the potatoes as they are placed in bags to be transferred to markets around the region. The producers tell us that the quality is unique in the area, not to mention the care taken in every stage of the process.

We find it particularly intriguing when someone explains that tunta depends on the frost. While this act of nature is usually associated with adverse events, here it is welcome. In Ilave, the potato-growing season is timed so that the harvest takes place around the time of the first frost, which occurs from May to July each year. In this complex, ancient process everything is related to the land, water, and air. Nature, potato, and man's role in the technique all play their parts, working together from beginning to end.

We continue, making a series of stops in the region, each one feeling like the exploration of some lost world. At Acora, Ernesto shows us how they collect *chaco*, an edible clay (hydrous aluminum silicate).

"We have always eaten bitter potatoes that are not the best," Ernesto tells us, "but we covered them with *chaco*, which doesn't cause any harm." Since pre-Inca times, chaco was used to provide nutrients (calcium and iron) in chile sauces called *uchucutas*, which would cover the bitter potatoes. Even today, chaco is consumed as an antacid by mixing it in a glass of water.

To obtain these small pieces of earth, called *ch'aqu* in Quechua or *passa* in Aymara (two of the indigenous languages of Peru), the locals manually dig pits, up to 5 meters (16 feet) deep, between May and December. Using a pickaxe—or their bare hands—they extract chunks of clay from the soil. Later the clay is left in the sunlight to dry.

We walk until the deep pits are at our feet. Around the edges the gatherers, who were here a few days before, have exposed pieces of dry clay. To remove the *chaco* that cakes the walls, we have to jump inside the pits. The clay is wet when we find it, but as we bring it to the surface, it dries and becomes stiff. Ernesto tells us to avoid the bluish or reddish clay as it contains other minerals. We know that there is much more if we keep digging deeper—how much more and for how much longer we don't know.

Further on, we pass by raised platforms called Waru Waru—ancestral technology used in flooded areas to help generate warm microclimates. The platforms can be up to 4 meters (13 feet) wide and 100 meters (330 feet) long. The water retains the heat captured from the sunlight during the day to protect crops from flooding. Waru waru helps extend the growing season, giving communities additional flexibility to adjust to the changing climate. Ernesto tells us, in great detail, of the plans to recover the Waru Waru in the region, as the practice has nearly died out.

North of Juliaca, at 3,800 meters (12,500 feet) above sea level, Genaro Ucharico, a local researcher, guides us to the fields of Vilque, where Andean grains like quinoa, *kiwicha*, and *kañiwa* are grown. While producers of *tunta* in Ilave wait in anticipation for the frost to start the process, grain producers are waiting with trepidation. Of the three grains, quinoa is perhaps the least vulnerable to the climate, thus the easiest to grow and—because of its high levels of protein (some varieties have as much as 22 percent)—the most popular. According to some reports, more than 3,000 varieties have been identified. As quinoa grows in popularity and the country, along with the rest of the world, is demanding a greater supply, scientists are focused on developing varieties that are pest-resistant and can adapt to different soils.

Still, these plants are vulnerable to the low temperatures of the altiplano. *Kañiwa*, due to its lower adaptability and high sensitivity to extreme climate and pests, sees much less production. An entire crop can be wiped out if farmers are not prepared.

Here they practice an ancient but new-to-us method called *canchones*, where parcels of land are raised like they are with Waru Waru, but instead of irrigation channels, they are marked with stonewall borders that capture the heat from the sun. Frost is less likely within these *canchones*, and with the increasing unpredictability of the seasons in the *altiplano*, production depends even more on these ancient farming practices.

Diversidad de quinuas

DIVERSITY OF QUINOAS

We create our own diversity of quinoas, less related to ecotype than their different colors. We continue the tradition of using natural dyes, seen in the textiles of the pre-Inca cultures of Peru, in our food. We never realized these dyes were something that could be so diverse and delicious. It's also a way to help us paint a Peruvian aesthetic—one that links the dish to the multitude of colors found naturally around us.

Serves 6

Quinoa leaves, 20 g
White quinoa, 300 g
Black quinoa, 100 g
Flaxseed oil, 40 ml
Airampo Dye (page 90), 10 g
Quinoa sprouts, 100 g
Llama & Chlorophyll (page 147)

- Run the quinoa leaves through a juicer to extract the chlorophyll and set aside.
- Working with one color of quinoa at a time, toast the white and black quinoa in a dry saucepan, then cover with 1 L water, bring to a boil and cook for 15 minutes. Remove from the heat and let stand, covered, for 30 minutes. Drain in a sieve and let cool.
- Divide the white quinoa into thirds. Mix one-third of the white quinoa with the chlorophyll and 10 ml of the flaxseed oil. Mix another one-third of the white quinoa with the airampo dye and 5 ml of the flaxseed oil. Leave the remaining white quinoa and mix with 10 ml of the flaxseed oil.
- Mix all of the black quinoa with 10 ml of the flaxseed oil.
- Spread the fresh quinoa sprouts and mix them with the remaining 5 ml of the flaxseed oil.
- Serve alongside the llama & chlorophyll; in small mounds separated by color.

Altiplano

Llama y clorofila

LLAMA & CHLOROPHYLL

We see the llama most often as a pack animal in the Andes, carrying loads from a harvest, such as sacks of grains or bundles of *ichu*, up steep mountainsides with ease. Unlike the alpaca, its wool is coarse and has little value. Llama is rarely eaten, though we can appreciate its milk and the rich flavor of a broth made from its bones. Here we try to see the llama in a different light, freely grazing on the green grass growing all around it on the high Andean plains.

Serves 4

Llama milk, 1 L
Cabuya molasses, 100 g
Llama shin, 3 kg
Quinoa leaves, 500 g
Peeled *cushuro*, 100 g
Sanky fruit, 1
Wild oxalis flowers, to serve

- In a pot, combine the llama milk and 50 g of the *cabuya* molasses. Bring to a boil over medium heat and cook, stirring, for 10 minutes until combined.
- Remove from heat and whisk the milk for 2 minutes; spoon off the foam onto a dehydrator tray and dehydrate at 70°C (158°F) for 20 hours until it forms a cracker. Break the cracker into irregular pieces.
- In a large pot, combine the llama shin with cold water to cover. Bring to a boil over high heat. Reduce the heat to the lowest possible setting, cover, and simmer the shin for 15 hours to melt the collagen from the shin—to obtain the gelatin. Strain the broth through a fine-mesh sieve, discard the meat and bones, and store the gelatin broth in the refrigerator.
- In a juicer, juice the quinoa leaves to extract the chlorophyll.
- In a blender, purée the *cushuro*, chlorophyll, and the remaining 50 g of the *cabuya* molasses until combined.
- Transfer the mixture to a saucepot and warm over medium heat. Remove from the heat and add the shin gelatin. Transfer the mixture to a tray and place in the refrigerator. Before serving, break it up into irregular gelee pieces.
- Peel the *sanky*, cut into 4 pieces, and place each on a plate. Serve topped with the gelatin, pieces of milk cracker, and wild oxalis flowers

El ichu

ICHU

Ichu are the tall, slender grasses that cover the *altiplano*, often seen growing wildly in patches and blowing in the intense winds. The *ichu* helps gives sustenance to camelids like the *vicuña* and alpaca. It's used as thatched roofing and insulation in many Andean homes, protecting families from the harsh climate. While seemingly irrelevant at first glance, *ichu* brings life to the altiplano.

Serves 4

Ichu, 500 g
Tunta, 200 g

- Prepare a charcoal fire until smoldering hot coals. Put the tips of the *ichu* stalks directly on the hot coals until charred.
- In a pot, bring 600 ml water to a boil and grate the *tunta* directly into the boiling water. Cook for 5 minutes, stirring constantly and vigorously, until it becomes a thick, white paste. It's important to stir forcefully, so there are no lumps in the mixture.
- Preheat the oven to 120°C (248°F). Line a 43 x 31 cm (17 x 12–inch) baking sheet with a silicone mat.
- Spread the tunta mixture on the lined baking sheet to a 1 mm ($\frac{1}{16}$–inch) thickness. Sprinkle the burnt *ichu* on top and bake for 30 minutes, or until it resembles a cracker.
- To serve, place a piece of the cracker alongside raw *tunta*.

Espesante de tunta

TUNTA THICKENER

Once the entire process of transforming a potato into *tunta* plays out, there are the logistics of transporting it to Central. The aroma does not come close to the intensity of *tocosh*, though somewhere between the collection and delivery to the restaurant, a sack of *tunta* will certainly result in an occasional unfriendly glance of a passerby.

We thought it would be impossible to incorporate *tunta* into the menu because of its funky, heady aroma. Weirdly, it reminds me of the time I was in charge of the cheese cart at The Ritz London. I was surrounded by French cheeses and at first, I hated them all. But gradually, surrounded by their constant presence, I grew to like them.

We had to do something like that with tunta to make it familiar. We tried to make it palatable to someone not from Cuzco, someone who did not have an emotional connection to *tunta*. We tried boiling it but were disappointed to learn that it destroyed the flavor—as well as its essence. Eventually, we developed a thin cracker that we then grated into a powder. We offer *tunta* in small doses, just the right amount.

Makes 500 g

Tunta, 1 kg, finely grated

- In a large pot, combine the grated *tunta* with 4 L water and, whisking constantly, bring to a boil over medium heat. Cook, stirring, about 10 minutes, or until the mixture thickens like glue. Remove from the heat and set aside.

CATEGORIES OF TUNTA QUALITY
I   Large, intense white, chalky, whole without cracks
II   Medium, bright white, whole without cracks
III Small, white or cream colored, whole or cracked
IV   Cream colored with yellow or black spots of various sizes, cracked

*Between categories II. and IV. the value begins to decrease and is intended for consumption by the producer himself, and not for the market.

DIFFERENT VARIETIES OF POTATOES USED FOR TUNTA
Bitter: Lucki, Locka, Ajamwira, Choquepito, and Parina
Sweet Natives: Imilla (black or white), Sani Imilla, Peruanita, and Plaita
Improved: Canchan, Ch'aska, and Perricholi

Arcilla de altiplano

ALTIPLANO CLAY

The driest areas of the *altiplano* are streaked with shallow pits where *chaco*, an edible clay, is collected regularly. There's plenty to go around. From a single visit to a pit, we can extract enough *chaco* to last us six months at Central. The clay is homogeneous and compact. Its consumption is nothing new in Andean communities. Used largely for medicinal purposes, it is known to protect the stomach lining, neutralizing toxic substances and astringents. For culinary purposes it is usually cured with salt, to make a sauce to mellow the sharp, bitter flavor of just-harvested potatoes. We understand its traditional association with the region's potatoes and often use them together in the restaurant's simulated *huatia* ovens, or to cover tubers that will be baked.

We also use the clay in sweet recipes, such as our creams, clay rocks, and clay ice. In short, this is an ingredient that has helped spawn more than fifty ideas at Central. Some were very good, some just okay, and others didn't work at all. Yet all of the ideas helped us chart a course to develop new recipes.

Serves 8

Milk Chocolate	Heavy (double) cream, 450 ml Milk, 450 ml Chocolate (70% Cacao Criollo), 900 g Cacao fruit pulp, 330 g	• In a saucepot, warm the cream and milk over medium heat. Add the cacao criollo and cacao pulp and let melt; stir to incorporate the ingredients. Set aside.
Chaco Clay Meringue	Egg whites, 220 g Cacao Crystals (page 240), 520 g *Chaco* clay, 30 g, pulverized	• In the clean, dry bowl of a stand mixer fitted with a whisk attachment, whip the egg whites on medium speed until soft peaks form. • In a saucepan, heat the cacao crystals to 120°C (248°F). Fold the melted crystals into the egg whites. Add the *chaco* clay powder, increase the mixer speed to high, and whip until stiff peaks form. • Line a 43 x 31 cm (17 x 12-inch) dehydrator tray with a silicone mat. Spread the meringue into the lined tray and dehydrate at 70°C (158°F) for 30 minutes until dry.

→ recipe continues on next page

Altiplano

Arcilla de altiplano

ALTIPLANO CLAY

Serves 8

Coffee Soil	Butter, 250 g Cacao Crystals (page 240), 250 g Egg yolks, 2 Sandia coffee, 50 g, ground Salt Dry potato powder, 200 g	• In a food processor, combine the butter and cacao crystals and process until creamy. Add the egg yolks, one at a time, then add the coffee and a pinch of salt, and process for 30 seconds until combined. Add half of the potato powder and process until smooth. Add the remaining potato powder and combine. Place the dough on a work surface and shape into a flat disk; wrap the disk in plastic wrap (clingfilm) and let it rest for 1 hour. • Preheat the oven to 180°C (356°F). • Place the coffee soil dough on a baking sheet and bake for 30 minutes, or until dry and firm. Set aside.
Herb Powder	*Muña*, 200 g *Marku*, 200 g Cacao Crystals (page 240), 600 g Butter, 540 g Egg yolks, 2 Salt, 2 g *Tunta* powder, 800 g	• Bring a medium saucepan filled with water to a boil. Blanch the *muña* and *marku* for 2 seconds, drain, shock in an ice bath, and transfer to a blender. Purée until a smooth paste forms. Set aside. • In a food processor, combine the cacao crystals and butter and process until creamy. Add the egg yolks, one at a time. Then add the herb paste and salt, and process for 30 seconds until combined. Add half of the tunta powder and process until smooth. Add the remaining *tunta* powder and combine. Place the dough on a work surface and shape into a flat disk; wrap the disk in plastic wrap and refrigerate for 1 hour. • Preheat the oven to 180°C (356°F). • Roll out the dough to a 1 mm thickness, and cut into irregular shapes. Place the dough on a baking sheet. Bake for 30 minutes until cooked. • Crush each of the baked doughs in a mortar; then combine the milk chocolate and *chaco* clay meringue separately. Place the "soils" in small mounds next to one another, divided by colors, on the dish until you get a nice, organic collection.

← recipe starts on previous page

Pseudocereales

PSEUDOCEREALS

We don't see the high Andes as a massive expanse of land for livestock to graze. Here, eating beef is unusual. Plant proteins have been providing what humans needed to sustain themselves well before the Spanish brought cattle. The arrival of cattle didn't have a significant impact on the Andean diet, as other animals have. However, its sacrifice is culturally relevant, as is evident when a cow is killed in an Andean village: It's an occasion to be shared by the entire community, an act that is very special, with many families taking part.

The Andean cow grazes among the fields of quinoa and all of the minty and bitter herbs: the *muñas*, *paicos*, and *huacatays*. Following in Andean tradition, we emphasize that eating meat at Central, though rare, should be a special occasion. We serve this beef surrounded by the same ingredients that the cow grazes—quinoa and wild herbs. Its food is ours as well.

Serves 4

Diversity of Quinoas (page 144)
Milk, 400 ml
Huacatay, 100 g
Paico, 20 g
Chincho, 15 g
Beef fat, 300 g
Bone-in beef short ribs, 1.2 kg
Dehydrated beef heart (see page 118), 70 g

- Cook the quinoas according to the method on page 144, but when you drain the quinoa, reserve the cooking water. Dye the quinoas as directed. You will end up with black quinoa, plain white quinoa, chlorophyll-tinted quinoa, and *airampo*-tinted quinoa. Set the quinoas aside.
- In a saucepan, bring the milk to a simmer over medium heat and cook, stirring, for about 10 minutes, or until the milk has reduced to half its volume. When the liquid reaches 60°C (140°F), remove from the heat. Add the *huacatay*, *paico*, and *chincho* in the milk and infuse for 1 hour.
- In a pan, melt the beef fat over high heat. Pat the meat dry, and sear the short ribs until nicely browned on all sides, about 30 seconds per side. Cover with the reserved quinoa cooking water. Reduce the heat to low, cover, and cook for 20 hours.
- To serve, strain the herb milk through a fine-mesh sieve. Pull the meat from the rib bones and plate. Place the beef in a mound over the plate, top with quinoas, and grate the dry heart over the top. Place the thickened milk alongside.

Pez de aguas de altitud

FISH OF HIGH–ALTITUDE WATERS

High altitude Andean lakes are full of life. They have rich ecosystems, much different from the coast, with fresh, pure water that comes traveling down from melting glaciers high in the Andes, helping fuel the farms in the surrounding valleys. The *pejerrey*, the smallish silverside fish, is commonly raised here, living amid the algae. Sheep graze along the shores and potatoes soak in wells beside streams to make *tunta*.

Serves 4

Pejerrey, 8
Coca leaves, 200 g
Tunta, 400 g
Flaxseed oil, about 2 L
Altiplano lake algae, 80 g
Sheep's milk, 320 ml
Salt

- In a smoker, smoke the *pejerrey* with coca leaves for 1 hour until it reaches 70°C (158°F) inside and 100°C (212°F) outside.
- Line two baking sheets with silicone mats. In a saucepot, bring 300 ml water to a boil. Grate 100 g of the *tunta* into the water. Stir constantly for 5 minutes until the mixture becomes thick and translucent. Remove from the heat and evenly spread the mixture over a lined baking sheet to a 2 mm (1/16–inch) thickness. Let it dry 1 hour.
- In a heavy-bottomed pot, bring the oil to 180°C (356°F) over medium heat. Carefully lower the whole *tunta* cracker into the oil and deep–fry about 5 seconds until crispy (don't let it brown).
- In a pot, combine the algae with water to cover. Bring to a boil over medium heat, reduce the heat to low, and cook the algae, uncovered, for 5 hours until soft. Transfer to a blender and purée until smooth. Transfer the algae purée to the other lined baking sheet and spread to a 5 mm (scant ¼–inch) thickness. Place a fan set to medium speed next to the baking sheet and dry the purée for 2 hours, or until you can touch it and it does not break
- Finely grate the remaining 300 g of the *tunta*. In a saucepan, bring the sheep's milk to 80°C (176°F) over medium heat. Add the grated *tunta* and stir slowly until smooth. Season the *tunta* purée to taste with salt.
- To serve, place all the smoked *pejerrey* on a plate, and top with the deep-fried *tunta*, the dried algae, and the *tunta* purée.

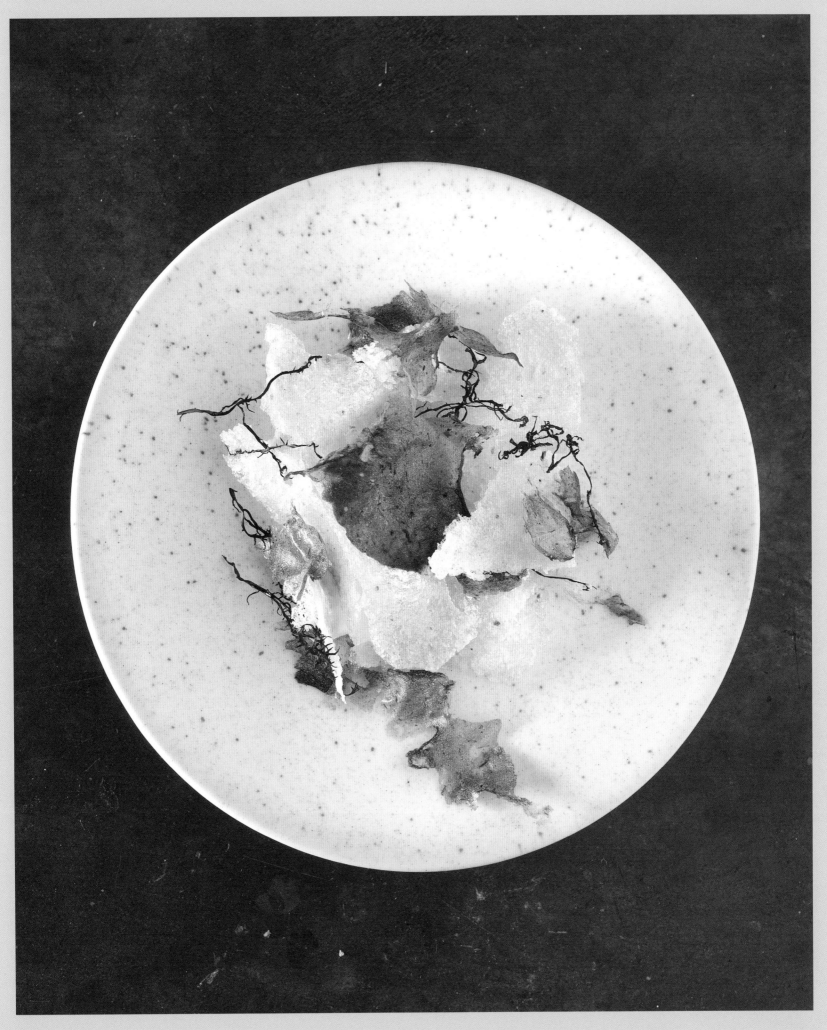

800 m · 2,625 ft

E
S
C
A
L
E
R
A

ESCALERA

The path through the *Cordillera Escalera* winds along a steep mountainside covered in lush vegetation. Sometimes we need to walk with our backs against the edge of the mountain so we don't fall. Eventually we come to a *sangre de grado (Croton lechleri)*, a tree with a bright red resin that looks like blood, and when you rub it on your skin, the resin becomes dense and milky, like pink latex. *Sangre de grado* has been used for centuries to heal wounds and cure gastric ulcers, which the locals call "stomach wounds."

The Cordillera Escalera is a conservation area in the province of San Martín, just outside of Tarapoto. It's high jungle, some of it cloud forest, a place with tremendous levels of biodiversity. There are bright orange Andean cocks-of-the-rock (*Rupicola peruviana*) and woolly monkeys (*Lagothrix lagotricha*), as well as orchids of different sizes, shapes, and colors. When you hear the word "rainforest," this is the image that comes to mind. Yet, very little research has been done on the local flora and fauna—and the deforestation is encroaching closer and closer, attacking the landscape from every side.

Our friend Cindy Reátegui recommended we come here. Her family runs a popular restaurant in Tarapoto specializing in the regional cuisine. She and her mother, Doña Elia, know and love this landscape like few others.

At the entrance to the reserve marked by a large *pomarrosa* tree, we meet with Pedro Tapuyimat. Tapuyimat comes from the indigenous Lamista community that, along with the Awarunas and Chayistas, settled here hundreds of years ago from the Andes. He knows the jungle like he knows the garden in the back of his house. We make stops every time he points out different species. Pedro can recognize and identify every species of tree, grass, and bush, as well as every flower and leaf, because he has been around them his entire life. The customs of his people include relying on these botanicals for their healing properties.

He teaches us about *chiriq sanango* (*Brunfelsia grandiflora*), the roots of which are steeped in alcohol and used for rheumatism; and *ajosquiro* (*Gallesia integrifolia*), for which he uses the machete to cut into the trunk releasing an intense garlic smell. There's *atadijo* (*Trema micrantha (L) Blume*) bark that's used to treat a dry cough; and the creeping vine, *clavo huasca* (*Tynanthus panurensis*), macerated in alcohol—to cure colds. There are curious resins in various trees. Some, like *huampo*, we know—and others we've never seen. We bring them back to the restaurant for testing.

Then there are fungi—light brown, cream, white, yellow, and orange, with rough surfaces and firm texture—on fallen tree trunks, where the humidity is concentrated. Most Peruvians call them *callampas*, a general term here for common wild funghi.

We pass several impressive waterfalls and see hundreds of shades of rocks in the Río Shilcayo, which we cross over a dozen times. Walking alongside a cliff, the ground is muddy and slippery—so we tread carefully. Pedro stands in front to show us a wild *bombonaje* plant (*Carludovica palmata*), an herb with stems up to 60 centimeters (24 inches) long, and with edible rhizomes and buds. The tender buds, which look like the edible heart of palm (*chonta*), have pearly white, elongated leaves.

Traditionally, the leaves are used to fashion hats, baskets, and fish traps. Despite having a nearly identical flavor to *chonta*, which is harvested unsustainably, no one outside of the region, that we know of, has ever tried to use it for culinary purposes. These plants grow fast and the buds can be removed without killing the plant. We wrap some in *bijao* leaves—as is done with chonta in Loreto to conserve it longer—to get it back to the restaurant.

After a humid, three-and-a-half hour hike through the mountains, we arrive at the house of a ranger. We eat and rest as the complete darkness of the night approaches and the distant sounds of wild animals grow closer. We set up camp on a small hill. Huge insects, including seemingly repellent-resistant mosquitoes, fly around our tents. We watch out for *isulas* (*Paraponera clavata*)—large black ants up to 4 cm (1½ inches) in length with extremely painful stings—that we had seen on a nearby cedar log.

The next day we awake before 6 a.m. to continue the journey. Following a refreshing swim at a waterfall, we agree to start the day's journey. We continue to climb up a zigzagging mountain path that is even greener and with more trees than our path the day before. Huge wasp nests and bulbous termite houses are attached to *ceibo* trunks. We had been using the trunks for support before realizing what a bad idea that was. Still, we have to chase Pedro, who at fifty-five years old is much more agile than we are. We stop, after a three-hour hike, in a small grove bordering a lagoon. There are mango trees, cacao, oranges, and *guanábanas* growing. The smell of ripe fruit entices us to take a rest and eat some fresh mangoes. We toss the skins in the lagoon for the fish.

Hours later, on our way down the mountain, our backpacks are full of souvenirs Pedro found for us. There are the *bombonajes* and resins, extracted from tree barks, in glass jars; chunks of branches and bark to be tested as decorations; and well-packed *ajosquiro* bark (to avoid getting the garlicky smell over everything). There are things we have never seen before or only read about, yet here they are in plain sight, waiting to be discovered by the wider world.

Gel de huampo

HUAMPO GEL

This resin extracted from *huampo* bark has become one of our favorite ingredients at Central, and is the basis for the Gelatina de Huampo recipe on page 172.

Makes 50 g

Huampo bark, 1 piece (50 x 12 cm / 20 x 5 inches)

- Brush any dirt off the *huampo* bark and cut it into 5 cm (2-inch) squares. Place the bark in a large pot and cover with 4 L water. Bring the water to a boil, reduce the heat to low, cover, and cook the bark for 4 hours, until the gel comes out. Strain through a fine-mesh sieve and cool completely. Transfer to a container, cover, and refrigerate for up to 3 days.

Masas de coca

COCA DOUGH

Escalera

It would be a mistake if we did not include coca leaves with their own recipe in this book. The value of leaves for many Andean communities and the power and spirit that they are connected to, is something to share. In the past we prepared a fluffier version of this bread, but because the flour and vegetable oil weren't from the region, we had to replace them with powders made from coca and corn, along with black quinoa. Now, the bread is very dense. Maybe we shouldn'teven call it bread.

Makes 30 pieces

Coca powder, 80 g (made from dried coca leaves)
Black quinoa, 80 g
Corn powder, 520 g
Salt, 25 g
Milk, 1.2 L
Butter, 300 g
Eggs, 2

- In a pot, combine 350 ml water and the quinoa, bring to a simmer, and cook the quinoa until tender, about 10 minutes. Remove from the heat, drain off the water, and set aside to cool.
- In a bowl, mix the rest of the ingredients with the cooked quinoa and add 70 ml water. Knead until a compact dough comes together. Let the dough rest for 1 hour 15 minutes.
- Preheat the oven to 260°C (500°F).
- Divide the dough into 80 g (3-ounce) pieces and shape into balls. Set aside on a baking sheet and let rest 10 minutes. Bake for 17 minutes. Transfer to a cooling rack and cool completely.

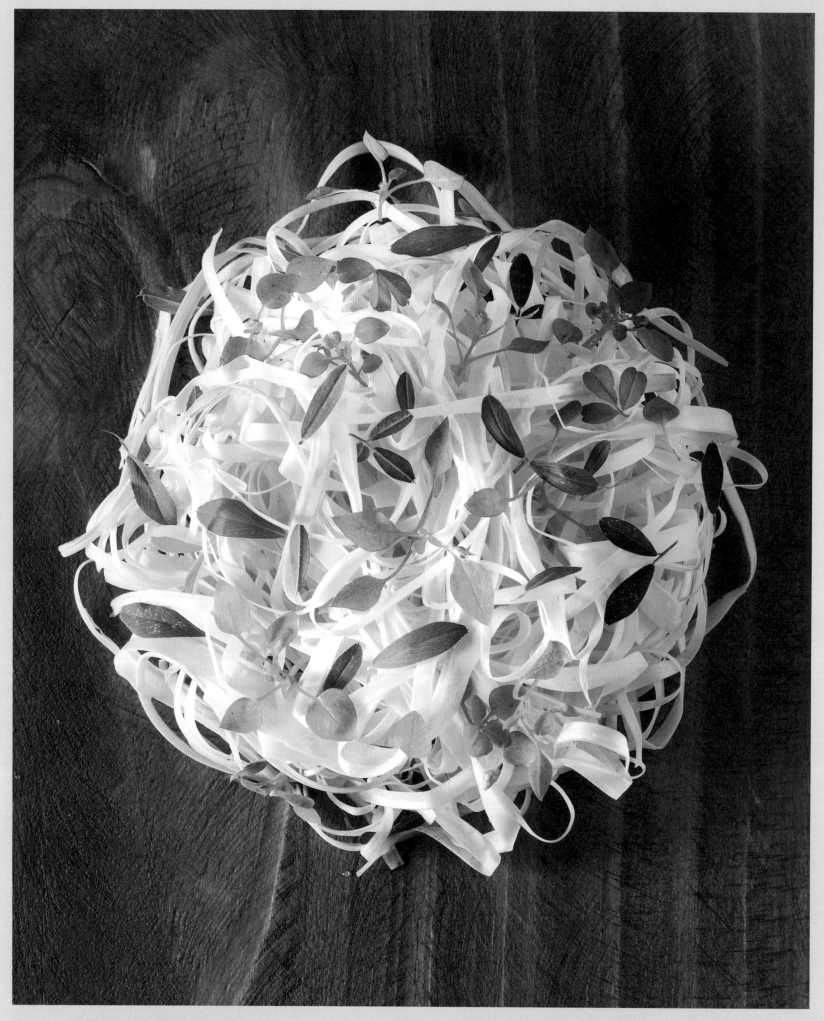

Escalera

Bombonaje

BOMBONAJE

We have found the *bombonaje* plant (*Carludovica palmata*) to be an ideal alternative for *chonta*, or heart of palm. *Chonta* has only recently become sustainably harvested by a few communities in Peru, though most chonta harvested here is extracted by cutting down the palm. However, tender buds of the fast growing *bombonaje*, have a similar look and flavor to *chonta* —and there's no need to cut down the entire plant.

Serves 4

Copoazú, 1
Sacha inchi oil, 30 ml
Bombonaje stalks, 2
Ruda leaves, 8
Hierba mala leaves, 12
Chincho leaves, 4

- Break open the *copoazú*, take out the pulp, and place in a bowl. Dress the fruit with *sacha inchi* oil. Separate the *bombonaje* stalks into threads and form into a circle, covering the *copoazú* mixture. Top with the *ruda*, *hierba mala*, and *chincho* leaves.

Gelatina de Huampo

HUAMPO GELATIN

One day, Karen Acevedo, a young woman from Chanchamayo who works in our pastry kitchen, and I were unpacking fresh cacao that just arrived from Palo Alto. It was the first shipment we had received from there, and, though we were very excited, we were careful not to break the fruit while removing the pulp from the beans. I told her about how the husk makes a great infusion. Karen began describing the infusions her community in the Selva Central used to make. They were mostly made with tree resin, from trees such as the *chuchuhuasi* (*Maytenus macrocarpa*), *capirona negra* (*Calycophyllum spruceanum*), and *lupuna* (*Ceiba pentandra*). Then she mentioned an infusion made with *huampo*, something her mother would drink before going to bed, and as she was describing it, I suddenly remembered tasting this special, glue-like infusion on a trip to Tarapoto, though I never knew the name. I wrote down the name and intended to go look for it on the next Mater trip.

Unbeknownst to us, Karen excitedly called her friends in the community and a few days later arranged to get several enormous pieces of *huampo* bark, which were almost as big as Karen herself. When she unpacked this giant box, it meant the world to me. And Karen was so proud to be sharing with us this small piece of who she is and where she comes from. *Huampo* was something she had around her all of her life, but she didn't think it would be of interest to us. We decided to use it right away.

Now, we get big pieces of the bark delivered to the restaurant. It's almost like we're getting an actual piece of a tree. The cooks break it into smaller pieces, and then let the pieces simmer for a few hours over low heat until the resin begins to float to the surface—the same method used by the locals. We try to get as much out of the bark as possible. We pour the liquid through a strainer and we're left with this clear gel, almost like a gum. The resin itself is not sticky and can even be used as a topical mosquito repellent.

We're incredibly fortunate to have people working with us from different regions. Just from a friendly, casual conversation, we found this incredible ingredient as well as access to extraordinary knowledge that we otherwise wouldn't have. Rather than us going to it, *huampo* came to us.

→ recipe continues on next page

Gelatina de Huampo

HUAMPO GELATIN

Makes 800 ml

Huampo Gel (page 164), 1 L
Cacao Crystals (page 240), 50 g
Muña, 1 bunch
Dale dale, 300 g, peeled
Stevia leaves, 15 g
Fresh turmeric, 2 g
Huacatay flowers, 2
Muña leaves, 2
Lemon verbena leaves, 2
Melissa leaves, 2
Fresh chamomile leaves, 10

- Combine half of the *huampo* gel with the cacao crystals and *muña* bunch and let steep for 1 hour. Strain and discard the *muña*. Transfer the infused gel to a 43 x 31 cm x 6 cm (17 x 12 x 2¼–inch) rectangular mold and place in the freezer until frozen, about 2 hours.
- Meanwhile, in a pot, combine the *dale dale* with 2 L water and bring to a boil. Reduce the heat to medium–low and simmer, uncovered, stirring, for 1 hour until it thickens. Remove from the heat and transfer to a blender. Add the remainder of the *huampo* gel and the stevia and turmeric and purée until smooth. Transfer the infused gel to a 43 x 31 cm x 6 cm (17 x 12 x 2¼–inch) rectangular mold and place in the freezer until frozen, about 2 hours.
- Grate the frozen *huampo* gel and place it on the *huampo-dale dale* crust. Top with *huacatay* flowers and *muña*, lemon verbena, Melissa, and chamomile leaves.

← recipe starts on previous page

Escalera

Amazonía roja

RED AMAZON

When I am in the kitchen with a *paiche* (*Arapaima gigas*), the biggest fish in Amazonía, I feel like this isn't a fish at all. It has a completely different physical structure. I cannot debone it like I would a grouper or sea bass. When I pass the knife under its scales there is one big, thick bone that splits the fish into two. I have to respect that the structure is unique to properly remove the flesh. Considering a single *paiche* can weigh as much as 400 pounds, it takes up a lot of room in the kitchen. The whole deboning area has to adapt. Right away, when you start to break it down, when you taste it and smell it, you know it's not from the sea. But it doesn't seem like it's from a river either.

Paiche seems more like a dinosaur than a fish, which, to some extent, is true. This Jurassic era fish breathes air and is covered with thick scales with a hard, mineralized outer layer. Also called *pirarucu* in Brazil, it lives in the shallow, muddy waters of riverbeds in the Amazon basin, rising for air every fifteen to twenty minutes for air. Though heavily overfished, it remains an important food source for indigenous œn communities. We used to get it wild until we realized it wasn't sustainable. Near Yurimaguas, a farm called Amazone, exports sustainably raised *paiche* around the world.

In this recipe we cure *paiche* with *airampo*, a wild cactus from the high jungle that dyes the flesh pink, and the result, visually, is almost like that of gravlax. Like the Shipibo that dye their skin with *huito*, we are trying to achieve the same thing.

Serves 4

Salt, 800 g
Airampo Dye (page 90), 300 g
Pacae Crystals (page 234), 300 g
Paiche (arapaima) fillets, 510 g
Red Oxalis leaves, 4 g
Chamomile flowers, 10
Ruda leaves, 4
Nasturtium flower, 1
Lemon verbena leaves, 4
Basil flowers, 4
Huacatay flowers, 4
Amazonian fish roe, 50 g

- In a deep container, mix the salt, *airampo* dye, and *pacae* crystals with 2 L water until combined.
- Place the fish in the marinade and refrigerate for 30 minutes. Remove the fish from the marinade and wipe the excess liquid with a damp cloth.
- Slice the fish 1 mm (1/16 inch) thin, and place on a chilled flat stone surface. Add the red oxalis, chamomile, *ruda*, nasturtium, lemon verbena, basil flowers, and *huacatay* flowers. Top with the fish roe.

Ollucos y cacao

OLLUCOS & CACAO

Cacao pulp has a beautiful fruity flavor that tastes very little like chocolate. However, if it is not eaten fresh, it is difficult to work with, since it oxidizes as soon as the pods are cut open, making whole cacao pods essential in this recipe.

Serves 4

Ollucos, 500 g
Cacao butter, 500 g
Cacao Crystals (page 240), 100 g
Cacao mucilage, 250 g
Cacao pods, 3

- In a saucepot, combine the *ollucos* and cacao butter and cook over medium heat to 65°C (149°F) for 5 minutes, or until soft. Drain the *ollucos* (discard the butter). Divide the *ollucos* in half and set aside.
- In a bowl, stir together the cacao crystals, cacao mucilage, and 100 ml water. Set aside.
- In a blender, purée half of the cooked ollucos.
- Open the cacao pods and remove the beans with their pulp. Carefully, to preserve the pulp intact, remove the cacao beans from the pulp and refill the holes left by the beans with the *ollucos* purée.
- To serve, place the stuffed cacao pulp and the cooked *ollucos* in bowls, and top with the cacao mucilage mixture.

Escalera

Cortezas

BARKS

In the Amazon there is a significant number of easy-to-find liquors and macerations. Often with cheerful or humorous names, the liquors use roots, bark, and herbs of the region for medicinal purposes, though most of them still go unnoticed by the world at large. The macerations, usually made using a sugarcane alcohol called *aguardiente* from the same region, are a way to preserve the roots and herbs. Sometimes the value we place on plants depends on our understanding of their relationship with local populations, and that can be quite profound. These people have so much knowledge about why the plants are here and what are they are for. They know their curative value and keep many of these tinctures around. It takes a lot for us to fully understand this relationship.

We normally use the barks of *sangre de grado*, *chuchuhuasi*, and *fierro caspi* to make macerations, though we'll also include some other roots and herbs that we find on our trips. We try to take in the wisdom of Amazonian healers, thinking about the combinations of plants that they might use, while using our intuition for how each preparation will come out. In Escalera, an area of steep inclines, we find tree and plant roots exposed by streams or erosion from rain. Their exposure allows us to choose the best ones among them.

After we make the macerations, which we use in our cocktail program, we usually keep the jars for just two weeks so they maintain a consistent flavor. The strength of the alcohol is always high, so we just use a small amount for the cocktail of the day, for sweets, or in a sour.

Makes 1 L

Yacuruna caspi bark (Croton cuneatus), 50 g
Catahua bark (Hura crepitans), 50 g
Chuchuhuasi bark (Maytenus nacrocarpa), 50 g
Cascarilla bark (Cinchona officinalis), 50 g
Tahuari bark (Tabebuia incana), 50 g
Fresh turmeric, 10 g
Aguardiente, 1 L

• Using a sharp knife, clean all the barks and peel the first layers. Place the barks in a glass jar, cover, and soak in the *aguardiente* with the turmeric for 2 months in a dark room.

Sanación

SANACIÓN

Escalera

Here we freeze ingredients that are often part of shamanic rituals, in which all elements in nature have a soul and a purpose. We freeze them to preserve the moment they were collected, and within this very water we maintain a balance of seeds, fruits, peels, barks, resins, and leaves that are part of this ancestral experience. What we put in is in relation to what we are using at that very moment. Usually we place roots with wood from Escalera on top of this.

230 m • 755 ft

A
M
A
Z
O
N
Í
A

230 m • 755 ft

AMAZONÍA

We awake at 5:30 a.m. to the smell of piranha and *doncella*, two common Amazonian fish, cooking over a wood fire. Though typical here in Paoyhan, a Shipibo community on the lower Ucayali River, it's an unusual breakfast for us. As in many rural communities, it's customary here to eat what you have on hand, and what they have is a snapshot of the region's biodiversity. On the pier we watch as canoes paddle in loaded with different varieties of bananas and *yuca*, as well as native fruits like *ungurahui*, *aguaje*, *cocona*, and *taperiba*. Then there are the fish, such as *gamitana*, *doncella*, *zungaro*, *machete*, and many others. Everything changes throughout the seasons.

Here in the jungle, life moves quietly. The stilted wooden houses, with roofs covered by dried palm leaves, are open, letting in the sounds of various birds, animals, and the wind in the trees. The hours of the day revolve around the climate, the season, and the need for food. Daylight is maximized, as common belief around here is that the night is full of dangerous spirits and mythical characters that can make you disappear into the forest.

We're here during the rainy season, and from the moment we climbed aboard a boat on the Ucayali and until we reached Paoyhan five hours later, the rain did not let up. We were offered hammocks in the house of Sr. Malhua, the shaman of the village. He's an elderly man, short in stature, with the courage of those who know everything you could ever need to know. Shipibo shamans speak of the need to connect the spiritual and actual worlds, which can be done through *ayahuasca*, a hallucinogenic brew prepared by the shaman. "He's the person who keeps watch," our Paoyhan guide, Gilmer Yuimachi, tells us of Sr. Malhua. "He maintains the peace and tranquility."

Native communities in this region tend to have an intimate relationship with their environment. Shipibo spirituality in particular speaks of harmony and balance, and, interestingly, about the reflection of heaven on earth. The geometric designs on their weavings and ceramics originate in the rainforest, from the skin of the anaconda, the Cosmic Serpent, the creator of the universe. Mothers even squeeze drops of liquid from *piri piri (Cyperus articulatus)*, a marsh grass, into their daughter's eyes, giving them visions for their designs that last a lifetime, and initiating them into the practice of their art. Their entire world revolves around the nature surrounding them.

Right now, the balance is out of whack in the Shipibo world. Illegal mining and logging in the Amazon are encroaching on their ancestral villages, and erosion and deforestation up and down the Ucayali have intensified weather changes. Cycles of severe droughts have killed many of the fruit trees around Paoyhan, and the heavy flooding that follows threatens the very foundation of the village. Some communities are forced to move from place to place, pushing them into a nomadic lifestyle.

The following morning we take a *peke-peke* (motorized canoe) two hours northwest, in the Tahuayo area, where Paoyhan could move to in the future. The water is dark and acts like a mirror against the trees and blue sky. Aquatic plants, which are eaten by other species—like the *taricaya*, a type of turtle—float on the surface. We disembark and walk into the forest. There are wide treetops with nearly ripe *pomarrosas* (rose apples). The intense fuchsia pistils are scattered on the forest floor over the dry leaves that creak with our footsteps, a sound that seems to echo. We find *limón rugoso*, *huicungo*, *ayahuasca* plants, towering *aguaje* palms, *huasaí*, superaromatic *taperiba* trees, and green *huitos* hanging from high branches.

We first came across huito in Iquitos a few years ago. It's the size of a passion fruit and turns brown when ripe. The flowers are very fragrant and are used in infusions to stop fevers. The bark is used as an astringent and anti-inflammatory, while the pulp is mostly consumed cooked. Communities prepare an alcoholic drink from it, called *huitochado*, or add sugar to make marmalades and jellies. What is most incredible is that when you oxidize the juice of an unripe huito, it becomes a shiny black dye. The Shipibo tattoo their face and bodies with the dye, as well as use it to dye their hair and textiles.

For us, it has become a beautiful, natural colorant to use in the kitchen. It's a way to paint the ingredients from this region with the colors that naturally surround them. To make it we have to grate the unripe pulp and the seeds into a kind of dust. It must sit for a moment in the fresh air to initiate the oxidization process, and then will go through two rounds of cooking over an extended period of time.

Another hour down river, we reach Cashibococha, a lagoon that was destined long ago, dictated by ancestral beliefs, to be used for fishing. It is believed that the village shaman has the ability to "control" the lagoon. For example, as a result of the shaman's strong connection with the natural world, fish like *paiche* may die in order to sustain the humans.

Fishing has always been one of the most important activities for the Shipibo. "The old men," says Gilmer, "fish freehand and use only arrows." Younger fishermen tend to use nets and wooden poles or sticks. Regardless, these methods ensure sustainable fisheries that can support local consumption. Only a small surplus will occasionally reach the market in Pucallpa.

At Cashibococha we learn how the fishing method works. We place wooden stakes into the water, arranging them at an angle, a "V," which are used to support the net. The fish get caught in the middle and we take in wild paiches of various sizes, plus a few *zungaros* and *doncellas*. The fish get divided up among the different families. Some place the fillets in salt, at a ratio of 1:1, preserving it for weeks. Others will cook their fish that day—fried, boiled, grilled, or wrapped in banana leaves.

At night, back at Paoyhan, the sky is clear and we can see the constellations clearly. We have been witness to a different lifestyle, of a place in the jungle with a distinct way of living. We can also see how ancestral customs are getting lost. The typical handwoven, brightly colored clothing is worn almost exclusively by the older Shipibo. New generations are migrating to cities, even though it often leads to even more hardships. They see their material possessions and modern clothing as a sign of progress, of a better quality of life; but as the outside world encroaches closer and closer around them, as their relationship with the natural world becomes more and more disrupted through no fault of their own, it's becoming more difficult to tell them that it isn't true.

El pez de las semillas rojas

Everyone thinks green is the color of the jungle, but it can be red, too. The river can be reddish, sometimes pink. Leaves fall from the trees, changing to red and brown as they dry, turning into food for the soil. There is also *achiote*, or *annatto*, the bright red seeds found inside a spiky fruit and used as a natural dye in many recipes in the region.

Serves 4

Bahuaja nut oil, 800 ml
Annatto seeds, 100 g
Gamitana, 2 kg
Annatto stems, 10
Annatto flowers, 5

- In a pot, warm the Bahuaja nut oil to 70°C (158°F) over medium heat. Add the *annatto* seeds, remove from the heat, cover, and let the oil and seeds rest until they cool completely. Cover and refrigerate.
- Debone the *gamitana*, and cover with the *annatto* oil in a deep container.
- Add *annatto* stems and flowers. Let the fish cure for 2 hours.
- To serve, thinly slice the fish and divide across 4 plates along with the oil and the aromatics.

El pez de las semillas rojas

THE FISH OF THE RED SEEDS

Carachama y yacón

CARACHAMA & YACÓN

While wondering through any market in the Northern Amazon one of the most striking fish you will encounter is the *carachama*. This smallish, armored catfish covered in thick black plates can be seen live in buckets of water or being grilled whole over charcoal. Fishing for *carachama*, as well as other freshwater species, is one of the main activities of the Shipibo-Conibo, the indigenous people who live along the Ucayali River. It's always done as a community, sharing whatever is caught. *Yacón* can be found growing near these fishing grounds.

Serves 8

Carachama, 1
Yacón, 1, peeled, (about 15 cm / 6 inches long)
Yuyo, 200 g
Yacón crystals, 110 g

- Clean the *carachama* and attach toothpicks to the fins so they stay stiff and open and to help maintain the natural shape of the fish, which will be used as a place to hold the yacón. Dehydrate at 70°C (158°F) for 20 hours; the skin and spines of this fish are very strong, so the dehydrated structure will be very sturdy.
- Preheat the oven to 74°C (265°F). Bake the *yacón* for 1 hour 30 minutes, rotating every 15 minutes. Then reduce the oven temperature to 93°C (200°F) and bake for another 30 minutes, rotating every 10 minutes.
- In a pot set over medium heat, combine the *yuyo* with 800 ml of water and bring a to a boil. Reduce the heat to medium and cook the liquid at a brisk simmer for 1 hour, until the liquid is reduced by about 70 percent of original volume and has a gel-like consistency. Strain the reduction through a fine-mesh sive and discard the *yuyo*. Set the reduction aside.
- In a small pot, combine the *yacón* crystals with 30 ml of water and bring to a boil. Add the dehydrated *yuyo* reduction and stir to combine. Set the syrup aside.
- To serve, slice the *yacón* and brush the slices with the syrup. Place the pieces on the *carachama* structure.

Amazonía

Sangre de árbol

BLOOD OF THE TREE

In San Martín we heard about these giant Amazonian snails, *los churos* (*Pomacea maculata*), which the local population eats as if they are river shellfish. With a hard, thick shell and blackish brown color, the snails inhabit lakes and lagoons, streams and wetlands—places with abundant vegetation. They can grow up to 16 centimeters (6 inches) in length in their natural habitat, and weigh up to 250 x. Its meat is considered of excellent quality as it contains a good amount of proteins and fats.

We also learned that larger fish swimming in the same Amazonian rivers, such as the *gamitana* (*Colossoma macropomum*) or *doncella* (*Pseudoplatystoma fasciatum*), feed on plants and fruits falling from the trees. These high-protein, low-fat fish with white flesh, popular with the Amazonian communities, are carnivorous too, swimming into smaller streams or flooded forests to feed on other fish and snails, including the *churos*.

In Paoyhan, we saw *churos* on a *sangre de grado* log floating on the surface of the water near a riverbank. *Sangre de grado* is a jungle tree from which we extract a resin of the same name. Perhaps this random encounter of churos on this particular tree had some significance? To complete a sense of place, we picked out flowers, plants, and seeds to add.

Serves 6

Ajosquiro bark, 50 g
Cassava Starch (page 64), 300 g
Puréed *sacha ajo*, 50 g
Chia seeds, 5 g
Doncella, 100 g
Honey, 200 g
Salt, 2 g
Churos, 6
Sangre de grado, 20 ml
Sacha inchi oil, 20 ml
Pensamiento (pansy) flowers, 8, julienned

- Bring 200 ml of water to a boil in a pot and then remove from heat, add the ajosquiro bark and cover. Allow it to infuse for 10 minutes, then drain reserving the infusion.
- Preheat the oven to 170°C (338°F). Line a baking sheet with a silicone baking mat.
- In a bowl, combine the cassava starch, *sacha ajo* purée, and the chia seeds, and knead together until a dough forms. On a flat surface, roll out the dough to a 2 mm (1/16–inch) thickness, and, using a paring knife, cut out irregular triangles. Transfer the triangles to the lined baking sheet and bake for 30 minutes. Don't let the dough brown. Set the cracker aside to cool.
- Meanwhile, fillet the *doncella*, cover with the honey and salt, and refrigerate for 1 hour. Remove the fish from the mixture and thinly slice. Cut the slices into roughly 6 x 6 x 3 cm (2½ x 2½ x 1–inch) irregular triangles.
- In a pot, combine the *churos*, 40 ml of the ajosquiro infusion, and *sangre de grado* and bring to a simmer over medium heat. Cook until the broth is reduced to a syrupy consistency, about 1 hour. Remove from the heat and let cool completely. Blend everything and combine the reduction with *sacha inchi* oil and, using a whisk, emulsify.
- To serve, cover the green cracker triangles with the cured *doncella*. Add the red *churo* emulsion, and top with the flowers.

Gamitana

GAMITANA

The *gamitana* (*Colossoma macropomum*), which some call *tambaqui* or *pacu*, was the first Amazonian fish we tried using at the restaurant that wasn't *paiche*. It eats everything it can find: smaller fish, shellfish, and fruits, like the *aguaje*, which we serve it with here. When we first tried it, we thought it was terrible: it was greasy and had lots of fat. We were left with this very earthy, fatty flavor lingering in our mouths for weeks. A year later we tasted it again, and realized that the first time around we had tasted an older *gamitana*; the younger fish are less fatty than the older ones.

Serves 4

Bombonaje, 300 g , cut into strips
Aguaje, 500 g
Sacha inchi oil, 100 ml
Amazonía cress
The Fish of the Red Seeds (page 192), using 300 g *gamitana*

- Arrange the *bombonaje* strips on a lined tray and dehydrate at 50°C (122°F) for 10 hours, until dry.
- In a pot of boiling water, cook the *aguaje* for 30 minutes, until soft. Drain, then peel and seed the fruit and transfer to a blender. Add 100 ml of *sacha inchi* oil and purée until emulsified.
- Place the *gamitana* on the plate with some dots of the aguaje purée, then cover with the Amazonía cress and *bombonaje*.

Pomarrosa

ROSE APPLE

The *pomarrosa*, or rose apple, is a part of everyday life in many Amazonian communities. The flowers cover the forest floor with carpets of fuschia petals, while the fruit has an amazing reddish pink color and a very thin, soft skin. The white pulp is sweet and refreshing, and the chamomile petals help support the delicacy of the fruit's flavor. The *aji dulce* adds even more color.

Serves 4

Ají dulce, 500 g
Pomarrosa fruit, 10
Egg whites, 60 g
Stevia Crystals (page 238), 10 g
Cactus Gel (page 74), 30 g
Lemongrass, 130 g
Papa voladora, 20 g
Fresh turmeric, 10 g
Maca root, 5 g
Chamomile petals, 200 g

- Clean the *ají dulce* to obtain the petals. Transfer the petals to a dehydrator tray and dehydrate for 10 hours at 50°C (122°F) until dry. Set aside.
- Peel the *pomarrosa* and place the skins in a dehydrator. (Set the fruits aside.) Dehydrate the skins at 40°C (104°F) for 2 hours, until dry. Transfer the skins to a tray and add the dried ají dulce petals. In a blender, pulverize the skins until combined. Set aside.
- In a blender, purée the peeled *pomarrosas* until smooth.
- In a clean, dry bowl, whisk the eggs whites until soft peaks form. Stir in the stevia crystals, *pomarrosa* purée, and cactus gel until combined. Transfer the mixture to the freezer and freeze for 3 hours until solid.
- Dehydrate the lemongrass in a dehydrator at 50°C (122°F) for 5 hours until completely dry. Transfer to a blender and process until a fine powder is formed. Set aside.
- In a pot of boiling water, cook the *papa voladora* for about 8 minutes, or until soft. Drain and transfer the *papa voladora* to a blender and purée with the turmeric. Grate the *maca* root into the purée.
- Line a 43 x 31 cm (17 x12-inch) dehydrator tray with a silicone mat. Spread the *papa voladora* purée on the lined tray and use an offset spatula to spread to a 2 mm (1/16-inch) thickness. Dehydrate at 60°C (140°F) for 3 hours, until dry; then break into small pieces.
- To serve, place a block of frozen *pomarrosa* on each of 4 plates. Sprinkle with the chamomile petals, lemongrass powder, *papa voladora* and *maca* crisps, and *ají dulce* powder.

Color de ungurahui

UNGURAHUI DYE

In Amazonian cities, the very nutritious *ungurahui* (*Oenocarpus bataua*) fruits are sold from baskets, shimmering in the sun like black olives. Though usually eaten fresh or in juices, we prefer to use it as a dye at the restaurant.

Makes 30 ml

Ungurahui, 1 kg

- Soak the *ungurahui* in 2 L cold water for 6 hours.
- Drain the fruit. Peel and place the pulp in a blender (discard the skin). Blend pulp until smooth.
- Transfer the purée to a saucepot and cook over low heat until the purée is reduced to one-third of its initial amount. Remove from the heat and pass trough a fine chinoise.
- Use immediately or freeze for up to 2 weeks.

Color de ungurahui

Amazonía

Tucunaré

TUCUNARÉ

Tucunaré, a type of peacock bass, means "friend of the trees" in Tupi-Guarani, as this ferocious hunter likes to hide within submerged roots and branches before it attacks its prey.

Serves 4

Shelled Bahuaja nuts, 800 g
Ungurahui pulp, 420 g
Sacha inchi oil, 100 ml
Tucunaré, 400 g
Sweet potato leaves, 500 g
Cassava Starch (page 64), 300 g
Bahuaja nut oil, 10 ml
Corn oil, 300 ml
Egg whites, 100 g

- Soak the Bahuaja nuts in water for 8 hours at room temperature. Remove the nuts from the water and finely grate.
- In a bowl, combine 700 g of the grated nuts with 1.5 L of warm water and let soak for 1 hour. Transfer both to a blender and blend until a smooth nut milk forms. Set a fine-mesh sieve over a bowl and pass the nut milk through it, pressing on the solids. Add 200 g of the *ungurahui* pulp to the nut milk and, using an immersion blender, blend until fully emulsified and foamy. Line a dehydrator tray with a silicone mat. Spread the mixture on a lined dehydrator tray and dehydrate the foam for 24 hours at 60°C (140°F).
- In a small bowl, mix together the remaining 220 g ungurahui pulp with the *sacha inchi oil*. Rub this mixture all over the *tucunaré*. Cover and refrigerate for 3 hours.
- Preheat the oven to 200°C (392°F). Line a 43 x 31 cm (17 x 12-inch) baking sheet with a silicone mat.
- In a pot of boiling water, blanch the sweet potato leaves for 2 seconds and shock in an ice bath. Transfer the leaves to a blender and purée with the cassava starch until smooth. Transfer the mixture to the lined baking sheet and using an offset spatula, evenly spread the mixture to a 1 cm (½-inch) thickness. Bake for 20 minutes.
- While the dough bakes, in a pot, heat the Bahuaja nut oil to 180°C (356°F) over medium heat.
- Remove the baked dough from the oven and carefully lower it into the hot oil. Deep-fry for 7 seconds until crispy. Set aside on a lined tray to absorb the oil.
- Heat the corn oil, to 70°C (158°F). Pour drops of the egg whites into the oil, and cook until the little spheres of egg white turn opaque. Drain and set aside for the plating.
- Prepare a charcoal grill. Cook the *tucunaré* fillet over the coals just on the skin-side until the skin is crispy. Remove from the heat and serve over the milk foam cracker, with the egg white spheres, Bahuaja nut dust, and coriander on top.

Color de huito

HUITO DYE

Amazonía

This *huito* (*Genipa americana*) fruit is sometimes eaten fresh or brewed into a tea, though throughout the Northern Amazon it is often used as a dye. The Shibibo-Conibos, Asháninkas, Machiguengas, and Tikunas use it to paint their bodies, to dye their hair, or to stain textiles. At Central, it's one of our favorite natural colorants to use in recipes.

Makes 500 g

Huito fruit, 3 kg

- Prepare a charcoal fire. Place the *huito* over the coals and cook until the skin is burnt. Remove the *huito* from the heat, then peel, grate, and transfer to a pot.
- Add enough water to the pot to cover the *huito* and bring to a boil over medium heat. Simmer, uncovered, for 3 hours until soft. Remove from the heat and strain through a fine mesh-sieve into a bowl, pushing on solids. Let cool completely, then cover and freeze for up to 2 weeks.

260 m · 853 ft

CHAZUTA

CHAZUTA

More than fifteen years ago the entire area around Chazuta was full of coca crops—which brought instability, turbulence, and poverty to the region. To combat the problems created by coca and to turn the region around, alternative crops were introduced. With the collaboration of the government and NGOs, farmers were asked to let the earth sit for three years, as coca had deprived the soil of all of its nutrients. Those that were patient planted cacao and coffee, and with a legitimate income from those crops, saw their lives quickly improve. In a short time, coffee and cacao became the preferred plants across the region. The farmers say with pride that they turned the white paste brown.

Chazuta is situated between the Cordillera Escalera and the Cordillera Azul National Park, on the left bank of the Huallaga River cradled between two forested hills: El Curiyacu and El Rompeo. The Huallaga, a major tributary of the Marañón River, anchors a vast valley with significant agricultural development, as is evident in Chazuta.

Mishky Cacao, which means tasty or sweet cacao in Quechua, is a cooperative of thirteen women who came together in 2003 to produce cacao. They are devoted to protecting their people and culture through an activity that creates jobs and promotes progress and tranquility.

Our primary contact with these women producers is Ms. Quinteros Ayli Cenepo, the president of this group. By phone Ayli is charming, with a sharp, assertive voice. She enthusiastically gives us directions and informs us that she and three other women from the group will sing us welcoming melodies of appreciation, happiness, and love—like they do every morning. These women radiate positivity.

We pass their small cacao-processing plant, a new building with many small, manual machines that require advanced technical knowledge. The Mishky have many dreams for their plant. They want to produce the best chocolate, though this represents a huge challenge.

After harvesting the cacao fruit, the women carefully, and with much effort, process the seeds, to make cocoa butter, paste, as well as jelly from the mucilage. They also grow *macambo* (*Theobroma bicolor*), a relative of cacao but with a larger fruit, which they process and experiment with, often combining the seeds with cacao.

While singing, they remove their newly made 70 percent cacao chocolate bars from the refrigerator. We catch a whiff of the sweet smell of cocoa butter, homogenized in a steel pan, and with this are encouraged to walk through the field. The fruit trees surrounding us are colorful and flavorful: *pomarrosas*, coconuts, mangoes, and *granadillas*.

Mishky's cacao trees are of varying sizes and grow on a slope amidst the aroma of mangoes, fallen fruit, and pink *pomarrosa* petals. The forest floor is covered with large, dried brown, red, and orange leaves. Fruit that falls to the ground ferments in a single day in this tropical climate. This mass of fermented leaves and fruits, mixed with unseen insects living within, serves as a natural compost.

With a sharp knife, we cut open a cacao fruit to reveal a cross section, just enough to expose the seeds. They're covered by a bright white pulp with a silky texture that's exquisitely sweet and refreshing. We pick up several fruits in each hand to take back whole to Central.

Cacao, as well as the entire genus of *Theobroma*, is said to have originated here in the Amazon basin before being traded up through Central America. Peruvian cacao growers have not yet had the success of Ecuador or Venezuela, though the industry is still developing. New wild strains are constantly being discovered in the region, each with its unique terroir.

We leave Chazuta at noon with the most intense sun blazing overhead. Passing the homes of the cacao farmers, we see a pond full of happy ducks feasting on *sapote* and *yacón*, both harvested in the area, and I hatch an idea for another dish. Further along we pass *shica shica* palms, which have menacing spines almost 10 centimeters (4 inches) long, that make the endemic species stand out in the forest. Its small round fruit, with red skin and a yellow-orange pulp—as well as a large seed that takes up two-thirds of the fruit—resembles an olive. A child in the area picks us two ripe *aperibas*. It isn't the harvest time for this fruit, so we're lucky to have them. We also collect some aromatic herbs, such as *sacha ajo* and *sacha culantro*.

The road is paved until we reach the fork to Tocache, at which a dirt road then leads to Pachiza to visit more cacao fields, ones growing at slightly higher altitudes than Chazuta, and we observe how mucilage from the fruit is obtained. A producer in Palo Blanco once sent a dark glass bottle to the restaurant; he gave us plenty of notice that it was coming. Carefully wrapped, with lots of protection, it was packed like a precious jewel. Inside the bottle was a dense, pinkish-white liquid: cacao mucilage. It was delicate and, because it fermented quickly, it needed to be packed, sent, and drunk without hesitation. We knew right away it was something special. Considering that whole cacao is difficult to find in Lima, we had to come to Pachiza to learn about the process.

Biologist Miguel Tam, from Loreto, guides us through the production of this juice. Once the pulp is removed from the beans, it gets pressed into juice. The liquid is then sieved, separating the pulp from a mucilaginous substance. He teaches us that about 20 percent of the pulp should be retained surrounding the bean, so it can continue its usual fermentation process to get the best results.

We see a new dimension to this fruit. For us, the pulp is more important than the beans because of the freshness. In the jungle, people pick a cacao fruit off a tree and cut it open with a machete in seconds. They chew the white part—the pulp—and spit out the beans. While the pulp is silky and delicious, the seeds are bitter. After hiking on a hot and humid day, it might be the most refreshing thing. As you taste it, you think *there's no way this is chocolate*—it's such a delicate fruit.

Working with the pulp is even more challenging than the beans: You need very fresh cacao pods. While you can transport cacao fruit rather easily, in the kitchen the pods quickly oxidize once they are cut open, so you need to work with them right away.

Despite this region being cacao's place of origin, until recently no one thought much about the plant or what the indigenous peoples have done with the fruit—or why. The native tribes didn't try to process the beans into chocolate—they didn't think it was anything special or worth pursuing. But now that they know it is special, there are communities across the region exploring what can be done with *Theobroma*. We are all learning. For such a well-known plant it's amazing how little we actually know about it.

Sapote, ungurahui y macambo

SAPOTE, UNGURAHUI & MACAMBO

Imagine walking through the forest with the sweetness of the fallen fruits enveloping your senses, and reaching down through the green plants to collect *macambo* seeds off the ground. This, essentially, is that dish.

Serves 4

Sacha culantro, 300 g
Milk, 1 L
Macambo beans, 100 g
Eggs yolks, 2
Cacao Crystals (page 240), 350 g
Cacao butter, 220 g, softened
Ungurahui Dye (page 204), 100g
Sapote (ripe), 400 g
Nasturtium flowers, to serve
Malvas flowers, to serve
Pentas flowers, to serve

- Preheat the oven to 120°C (248°F). Line a baking sheet with a silicone mat.
- In a pot of boiling water, blanch the *sacha culantro* for 3 seconds. Drain, transfer to a blender, and blend to obtain a thick paste. Spread the paste on the lined baking sheet to a 1 mm (1/16–inch) thickness. Bake for 10 minutes until dry. Transfer the cracker to a cooling rack and let cool until crispy.
- In a pot, combine the milk and *macambo* and warm over medium heat. In a bowl, beat the egg yolks with 200 g of the cacao crystals until combined. Beat some hot milk mixture into the yolk mixture to temper it, then pour the custard into the pot. Return the pot to low heat and cook, stirring, for 10 minutes until thick. Remove from the heat, transfer the custard to a Pacojet beaker, and freeze.
- In a saucepan, melt the remaining 150 g cacao crystals over medium heat. Mix the softened cacao butter with the melted cacao crystals and the *ungurahui* dye. Cool in a cylinder mold that is 15 cm (6 inches) high and 6 cm (2½ inches) in diameter.
- Using a vegetable peeler, shave ribbons from the molded *ungurahui* mixture.
- Peel the *sapote* and remove its pulp. Using a blender, purée the pulp and spread it in the lined tray. Dehydrate the pulp for 5 hours at 60°C (140°F) until dry.
- When ready to serve, pass the macambo–cacao ice cream through the Pacojet.
- Place a scoop of the macambo–cacao ice cream in each bowl and cover with the *sacha culantro* crackers, *ungurahui* shavings, *sapote* sheets, and roasted macambo.

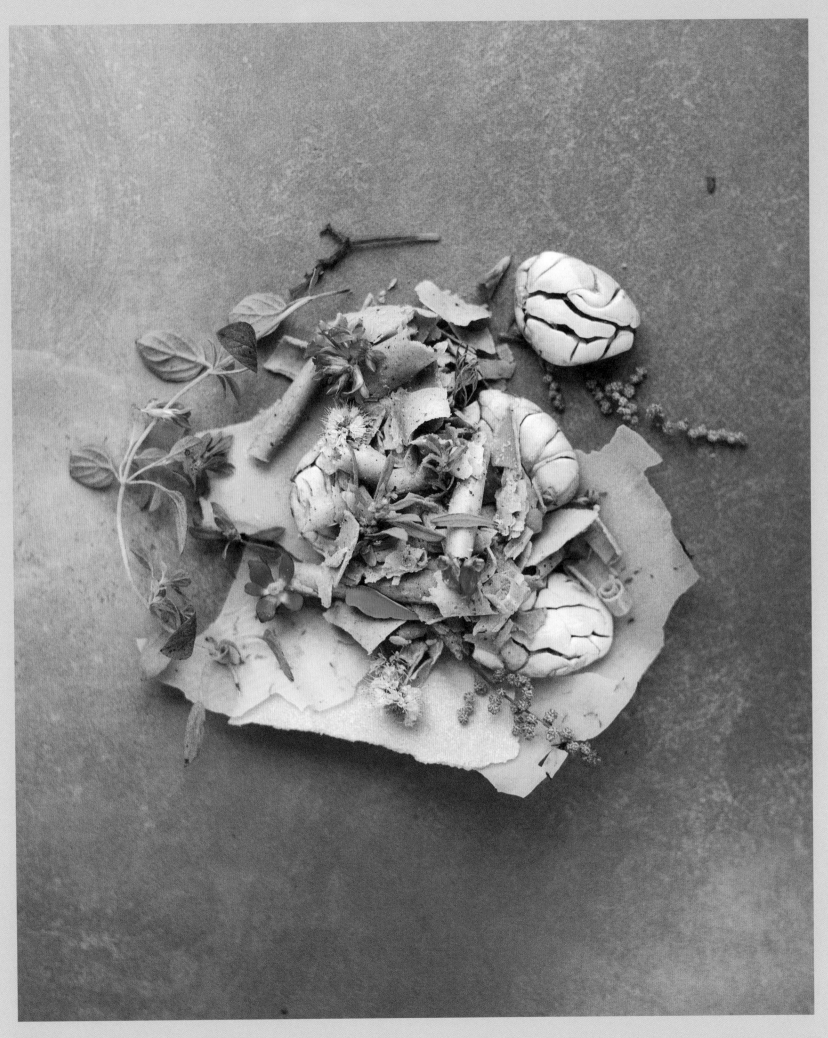

Miel en la jungla

HONEY IN THE JUNGLE

We have been pairing *cocona* and honey in our sweets since the very first days of Central. The idea has since evolved in many ways. Though the two ingredients have always been a part of the altitude menu, the textures, recipes, and our particular uses have changed. *Cocona* (*Solanum sessiliflorum*) is a well-known, oversized orange-yellow berry, and its cultivation in Chazuta is fairly large. *Cocona* is intensely tart and sweet, and to balance it out there is no better pairing than honey from the region. The infusion of various barks or leaves adds a spiritual and medicinal facet to the final dish.

Serves 4

Cocona purée, 300 g
Honey, 400 g
Huampo Gel (page 164), 200 g
Graviola leaves, 50 g

- In a pot, combine the *cocona* purée with 150 g of the honey and 100 g of the *huampo* gel. Set the pot over medium heat and cook until the mixture is reduced to half of its original volume.
- In another pot, on medium heat, make an infusion with the *graviola* leaves for 6 minutes at 70°C (158°F), then mix with the remaining 250 g of honey, and reduce to one-third of its original volume. Mix in the remaining 100 g of *huampo* gel and let cool.
- On a 43 x 31 cm (17 x 12-inch) rimmed baking sheet or tray, spread the *cocona*-honey reduction and refrigerate for 3 minutes. Pour the graviola-honey mixture on top and refrigerate for 2 hours until solid.
- To serve, cut the mixture into 1.5 x 15 cm (⅔ x 6-inch) strips.

Raiz yacón y pato

YACÓN ROOT & DUCK

Sometimes the creation of a course is simply seeing the components all together. That was the case when we were traveling to a friend's farm outside of Tarapoto. Ducks were flying over a lake surrounded by green vegetation. Around us were *shimbillo* trees and an orchard of mangoes, *sapotes*, and other fruits beside a farm full of colorful *mashuas* and *yacón*.

Serves 4

Skinless, boneless duck breast, 1
Shimbillo bark, 300 g
Fresh turmeric, 30 g
Yacón, 1, cut into rectangles
Hierba buena, 10 g
Heavy (double) cream, 120 ml
Mashua leaves, 4
Mashua, to serve
Chazuta cress, to serve

- In a smoker, smoke the duck breast with the *shimbillo* bark. Cook until the external temperature of the duck reaches 110°C (230°F) and the internal temperature reaches 75°C (167°F).
- In a pot, bring 400 ml water to a simmer over medium heat. Add the turmeric and cook for 20 minutes. Remove from the heat, add the *yacón* and *hierba buena*, and let sit for 30 minutes.
- In a blender, blend 200 g of the smoked duck with the cream until smooth. Pass through a fine-mesh sieve into a bowl, pressing on the solids. Set aside.
- Drain the *yacón* and reserve the turmeric liquid for another use.
- To serve, put the smoked duck cream on one side of a *yacón* rectangle and wrap the rectangle in *mashua* leaves. Spoon more of the duck cream on one side of the wrapped *yacón* and top with the pieces of *mashua* and Chazuta cress.

Chazuta

Papa voladora

FLYING POTATO

In the country with the greatest diversity of potatoes, it is ironic to speak of a species that differs greatly from all of the others, and yet can be used in much the same way. The appearance, shape, and texture—not to mention the skin color—are drastically different from any potato you have ever seen. Called the flying potato, it grows suspended in the air, on a climbing plant that can grow up to three meters (ten feet) tall. It's strange to see this plant for the first time. Most imagine a tuber growing under the earth for the entirety of its life. Suddenly, an outstretched arm harvests a potato right out of the air. Sharing the same soil, or rather air, of the potato vine are *huito* fruit, *annatto* (used as oil), and *Bahuaja* nuts, which we use to strengthen the sense of the surrounding ecosystem.

Serves 4

Papa voladora, 1 kg
Bahuaja nut oil, 120 ml
Salt, 2 g
Annatto seeds, 30 g
Papa voladora starch, 20 g
Huito Dye (page 210), 10 g
Verbena
Verbena flowers

- Steam the *papa voladora* for 20 minutes over simmering water. Remove from the heat and peel the potatoes while they are still hot. Cut half the potatoes into small dice.
- In a pan set, warm 30 ml of the nut oil over medium heat. Add the diced potatoes, season with salt, and sauté for about 6 minutes, or until golden.
- In a blender, combine the remaining potatoes with 20 ml of the nut oil and salt and purée on medium speed for 3 minutes, to 70°C (158°F).
- Mix the *annatto* with the *papa voladora* starch to form a paste and cook it for 30 minutes over low heat. Remove the mixture from the heat, spread thinly on a silicone mat–lined tray, and dehydrate for 1 hour at 40°C (104°F) until dry. Paint irregular lines with the *huito* dye, return to the dehydrator, and dry at 40°C (104°F) for 30 minutes, or until the huito dye is dry. Let cool; then break into pieces
- Dehydrate the verbena and verbena flowers at 30°C (86°F) for 3 hours until dry.
- To serve, place *papa voladora* purée on the plate, top with the sautéed *papa voladora*, and cover with *annatto* crackers.

Frutas, semillas y chocolate

FRUITS, SEEDS & CHOCOLATE

We felt we had to translate the feeling of walking on Amazonian soil where we constantly would find fruit that had fallen from trees along with seeds that blew in with the wind. There are flashes of greens, browns, and distinct tones of white. It all gets combined with an ingredient that we immediately connect with the forest: cacao.

Serves 8

Banana purée, 500 g
Banana powder, 150 g
Bahuaja nut oil, 5 ml
Hierba buena, 20 g
Taperiba fruit, 20 g
Cacao beans, 10 g
Chocolate (70% cacao criollo), 300 g
Chia seeds, 15 g

- Preheat the oven to 180°C (356°F).
- Mix the banana purée with the banana powder. Grease a 43 x 31 cm (17 x 12–inch) baking sheet with the nut oil and spread the banana mixture over the sheet. Bake for 15 minutes, or until golden. Remove from the heat and set aside.
- In a pot of boiling water, blanch the *hierba buena* for 3 seconds and shock in an ice bath. Drain and process in a blender until a thick paste forms. Line a dehydrator tray with a silicone baking mat. Spread the paste on the lined tray and dehydrate at 35°C (95°F) for 4 hours until dry.
- Peel the *taperibas* and discard the skin. Take the remaining pieces and dehydrate for 48 hours at 50°C (122°F) until dry.
- Crush the dried pieces and combine in a blender with the banana mixture, *hierba buena* paste, and cacao beans.
- Melt and temper the chocolate. Divide the tempered chocolate across 8 bowls. Sprinkle all the ingredients on the top, including the chia seeds.

Chazuta

Madera y cacao

WOOD & CACAO

In the green mountains, the smell of wet wood on fallen logs and branches is reminiscent of cocoa beans fermenting in enormous wooden containers. The first time we saw dry cacao beans, we thought about how similar they were to the colors of the rainforest barks. They too are full of colors and textures, adding different tones of white and brown, with dark veins running through them, layered in multicolored lichens.

Serves 4

Cacao pulp, 400 g
Egg whites, 600 g
Chuchuhuasi bark, 10 g
Cacao beans, 20 g
Fresh turmeric, 20 g, grated
Ungurahui, 20 g, grated
Cassava Starch (page 64), 30 g

- Spread 300 g of the cacao pulp on a dehydrator tray and dehydrate at 60°C (140°F) for 56 hours, until hard. Transfer to a blender and pulverize until a fine powder forms.
- In a clean, dry bowl, beat 200 g of the egg whites until they double in volume. Add the remaining 100 g cacao pulp and beat for 3 minutes until well incorporated. Fold in the cacao pulp powder and freeze the mixture in a tray for 5 hours until frozen.
- In a pot, combine one-third of the bark, the cacao beans, and 300 ml water and bring to a boil over high heat. Reduce the heat to low and simmer for 10 minutes. Remove from the heat and let sit for 15 minutes. Strain through a fine-mesh sieve and set aside.
- In another pot, combine one-third of the bark, the turmeric, and 300 ml water and bring to a boil over high heat. Reduce the heat to low and simmer for 10 minutes. Remove from the heat and let sit for 15 minutes. Strain through a fine-mesh sieve and set aside.
- In a third pot, combine the remaining bark, the *ungurahui*, and 300 ml water and bring to a boil over high heat. Reduce the heat to low and simmer for 10 minutes. Remove from the heat and let sit for 15 minutes. Strain through a fine-mesh sieve and set aside.
- Line three 43 x 31 cm (17 x 12-inch) dehydrator trays with silicone mats. Once the infusions are ready, add 10 g of cassava starch to each infusion to thicken the liquid. Place the liquids in the dehydrator trays and dehydrate at 75°C (167°F) for 3 hours until dry; then break into small pieces.
- To serve, place 3 irregular pieces from the frozen cacao pulp in each of the 4 bowls and sprinkle each with small amounts of different dried infusions.

Cristales de Pacae

PACAE CRYSTALS

Instead of sugar, we use different ingredients to convey sweetness as well as a sense of place. There is a reason we have chosen each ingredient—perhaps because of its origin, or maybe its story, or other quality.

Makes 60 g

"Cotton" from *pacae* pods, 300 g
Cassava Starch (page 64), 10 g

- In a high-powered blender, combine the *pacae* cotton and 400 ml water and process for 3 minutes at medium-high speed. Pass through the Superbag 2 times.
- Pour the *pacae* juice into a bowl and sprinkle in the starch. Using an immersion blender, mix on low speed until is completely dissolved with no lumps remaining.
- Line a 43 x 31 cm (17 x 12-inch) dehydrator tray with a silicone mat. Transfer the *pacae* liquid to a saucepan and set over medium heat. Stirring constantly with a silicone spatula, bring the liquid to 98°C (208°F). Pour the liquid onto the lined tray and evenly spread to a 1 mm (⅟₁₆-inch) thickness using a spatula. Transfer to a dehydrator and dehydrate at 75°C (168°F) for 36 hours. Once dry, break the sheets in a mortar and grind to the desired coarseness.

Cristales de huarango

HUARANGO CRYSTALS

The *Prosopis limensis* has become a tree species we feel extremely close to. For example, we found a *huarango* just blocks from the restaurant, and with almost every trip we find ourselves in the shadow of another one, protecting us from the sunlight. The huarango is native to the Ica region, where it is used by local communities for syrup. Deciding to make *cristales* from huarango seemed like a natural fit. It has some other notes mixed in: bitterness, acidity, with hints of coffee and smoke as well.

Makes 40 g

Huarango molasses, 200 g
Cassava Starch (page 64), 14 g

- Line a 43 x 31 cm (17 x 12–inch) dehydrator tray with a silicone mat.
- In a saucepan, combine the molasses and starch and cook over low heat until the syrup reaches 88°C (180°F). Remove from the heat, pour the syrup onto the lined tray, and spread to a 2 mm (1/16–inch) thickness. Place the tray in a dehydrator and dehydrate at 63°C (145°F) for 48 hours. Using a mortar and pestle, break into desired size pieces.

Cristales de stevia

STEVIA CRYSTALS

Stevia now grows across various parts of Peru, but it wasn't until a few years ago that anyone realized this sweet green leaf can thrive here in the Amazon and high Andes. Originally from Paraguay, it has been used historically by the Guaraní as a sweetener for *mate*, and the leaves themselves were chewed for sweetness. What a contradiction it is to be talking so much about rediscovering (and discovering) Peruvian ingredients while offering little white packets to patrons to sweeten their coffee. Offering stevia was a start, but we had to come up with something that was more to do with the plant. We began making syrups, infusing the fresh leaves we managed to grow in our garden even though the plant simply does not at all belong on the coast. After making syrup, we thought to make crystals as a way to measure the strength of the dosage and the intensity of the sweetness, not to mention to preserve it longer and maintain its quality.

Makes 100 g

Stevia leaves, 65 g
Cassava Starch (page 64), 4.5 g

- In a bowl, combine the stevia leaves with 450 ml water. Using an immersion blender, gradually add the starch until fully incorporated. Transfer the mixture to a pot and set over medium heat. Stirring constantly, bring the mixture to 98°C (210°F), and let it rest for 5 minutes, covered.
- Meanwhile, line a 43 x 31 cm (17 x 12-inch) dehydrator tray with a silicone mat.
- Remove the syrup from the heat and transfer to the lined tray. Using an offset spatula, thinly spread the syrup to a 1 mm (1/16-inch) thickness. Transfer the tray to a dehydrator and dehydrate at 75°C (167°F) for 36 hours, or until dry.
- Using a mortar and pestle, break the dried syrup to desired-size chunks. Keep in a dry, covered container at room temperature for up to 2 weeks.

Cristales de yacón

YACÓN CRYSTALS

By now it should be clear that we are fascinated by ingredients that are physically close to the ground. The *yacón* root is special not only because it grows under the ground, but also because of the incredibly smooth texture, high water content, and sweetness of its pulp—making it an extremely versatile ingredient in different recipes. The crystal form allows us to store it in a dry airtight box and sprinkle it in a recipe just like with sugar.

Makes 80 g

Yacón, 2 kg
Cassava Starch (page 64), 7g, sifted

- Peel the *yacón* and pass through a juice extractor; then strain through a fine-mesh sieve, pressing on solids.
- Transfer the juice to a saucepan and bring to a simmer over medium heat. Reduce the juice to one-fifth of its original volume. Little by little, add the starch, and mix on medium speed with an immersion blender until all is combined. Take the liquid up to 92°C (197°F).
- Meanwhile, line a 43 x 31 cm (17 x 12–inch) dehydrator tray with a silicone mat.
- Spread the yacón mixture on the lined tray to a 2 mm (⅟₁₆–inch) thickness. Transfer to a dehydrator and dehydrate at 75°C (167°F) for 6 hours until dry. Keep in a clean, dry container, covered, until ready to use.

Cristales de cacao

CACAO CRYSTALS

Crystals

We sweeten cacao with cacao. This fruit has so many uses and offers so many possibilities. Obtaining mucilage from cacao can be an exhausting task, but it is well worth it. In the Chazuta chapter (page 216), we talk about our experience in San Martín and visits to cacao growers. Despite appearing relaxed about everything, the growers are thorough people, striving for perfection when processing cacao beans and they are eager to share their methods.

It is from them that we have learned about the byproducts of cacao fruit, like the mucilage and the pulp—and this knowledge opened another door for us. Cacao pulp— which we use to make the crystals—is what these growers identify with (rather than the chocolate itself), drawing upon childhood memories of playing with the fruit, picking it off the tree, and drinking cacao pulp juice for breakfast.

Makes 80 g

Cacao pods, 2
Cassava Starch (page 64), 7 g

- Break the cacao pods and remove all the white "meat" in the center (where the beans are). Transfer the pulp-covered beans to a bowl. Cover the beans with 100 ml water (or enough to cover) and squeeze the beans with your hands until all the beans are removed from the pulp. (Set the beans aside for another use.) With an immersion blender, mix the clean white pulp with the starch.
- Line a 43 x 31 cm (17 x 12-inch) dehydrator tray with a silicone mat. Transfer the cacao pulp mixture to a saucepan and warm, stirring, to 98°C (210°F) over medium heat. Spread the hot mixture in the lined tray to a 3 mm (⅛-inch) thickness. Transfer to a dehydrator and dehydrate at 75°C (167°F) for 48 hours until dry. Using a mortar and pestle, break the cacao crystals into small pieces. We use this as a natural sweetener for different recipes.

G L O S S A R Y

ABUTA
Abuta grandifolia
This Amazonian tree in the Menispermaceae family grows in humid, tropical areas in the Upper Amazon. Its bark, leaves, and roots are used in infusions or macerations for medicinal purposes.

ACHIOTE / ANNATTO
Bixa orellana
This small tree (3–5 meters /10–16 feet high) has oval-shaped fruit and bright red seeds that contain bixin, a pigment used for coloring skin, fabric, and foods. It is also called annatto.

AGUAJE
Mauritia flexuosa
One of the most abundant palm trees in the Amazon, aguaje is also called moriche, canangucho, or buriti elsewhere in the region. The fruit has an oval shape; a reddish, hard, scaly skin; and a yellow, creamy pulp surrounding the seed. The pulp is high in Vitamin C and is often used to make juices, jams, or ice cream.

AGUARDIENTE
In Peru, aguardiente generally refers to a spirit distilled from sugarcane juice, mostly in rural villages. It is primarily made in small batches and not for sale commercially.

AGUAYMANTO
Physalis peruviana
Also known as the cape gooseberry, this yellow-orange cherry-size fruit is native to the high tropics of Peru, Ecuador, and Colombia. It has high levels of vitamin C and has a sweet and tangy flavor that makes it ideal for desserts, sauces, and jams.

AIRAMPO
Opuntia soehrensii
Growing in highland regions above 3,000 meters (9,842 feet) above sea level, this oval-shaped, purple- or fuchsia-colored cactus fruit is 5–8 centimeters (2–3 inches) long, with an intense fuchsia-colored pulp. Its bright purple seeds are used as a colorant for food and fabrics, as well as in infusions for medicinal purposes.

AJÍ AMARILLO
Capsicum baccatum
A capsicum in the Solanaceae (nightshade) family, ají amarillo is a moderately spicy Peruvian chile that becomes orange upon reaching maturity. It has a unique and aromatic flavor and is used in many traditional Peruvian recipes. After being dried in the sun, it is called ají mirasol.

AJÍ CHARAPITA
Capsicum frutescens
Originating in South America's northern Amazon regions, this tiny yellow pepper, also called ají charapa, is one of the spiciest in Peru. It's often mixed with cocona fruit to make a chile sauce or used in Amazonian ceviches.

AJÍ LIMO
Capsicum baccatum
This is a variety of chile that can be rounded or elongated. It may be green, red, yellow, orange, or purple. Spiciness is pronounced and tasty.

AJÍ PANCA
Capsicum baccatum
This mild dried chile, with a fruity, almost berry-like flavor with hints of smoke, changes in color from green or yellow to dark red or chocolate brown as it matures. It is usually sold whole or as a paste.

AJOSQUIRO
Gallesia integrifolia
This evergreen tree grows in lowland tropical areas of Peru and Bolivia. When cut, the leaves or any surface of the tree smells intensly of garlic. An infusion of its bark or leaves is used to cure fevers.

ALGARROBO
Prosopis pallida
This is an endemic tree from the warm tropical northern coastal area of Peru. Ecologically, the algarrobo is essential for its role as a water reservoir and its support of desert plant life. The tree produces pods used to make a rich, aromatic syrup, called algarrobina, to glaze meats or for cocktails.

ANCHOVETA
Engraulis ringens
This marine fish, which average about 20 centimeters (8 inches) in length is found mainly within 80–160 km (50–105 miles) of the coast, forming huge schools, chiefly in surface waters. Its distribution is entirely dependent on the rich plankton of the Humboldt Current. Used primarily for fishmeal, it is the most heavily exploited fish in world history.

ARRACACHA
Arracacia xanthorrhiza
Cultivated in Peru between 2,000 and 3,800 meters (6,560 and 12,467 feet) above sea level, this Andean plant, from the same family as carrot and celery, has a nutritious starchy root high in beta carotene. It can be boiled, fried, used in stews or desserts, and has a sweet flavor and creamy texture when cooked.

ATADIJO
Trema micrantha
Sometimes called the Jamaican nettletree, this small flowering tree is native to tropical areas of most parts of the Western hemisphere. In Peru, indigenous Amazonian communities use the bark in infusions to treat a dry cough.

AYAHUASCA
Banisteriopsis caapi
Originating in the Amazon rainforest, this psychoactive vine in the Malpighiaceae family is prepared with other native plants by indigenous shamans. The objective of the ayahuasca ceremony is to connect the souls of men and nature in order to enter the spiritual world. It is believed that taking part in this ritual can heal physical illnesses and restore spiritual balance.

AYASISA
Tagetes erecta
Also known as calendula, or in Amazonian shamanism as rosa sisa or flor de la muerte (flower of death), this aromatic flowering plant, a variety of marigold, grows year round in Peru's Andes and Amazon. Its heady herbal leaves and flowers are used medicinally to help cleanse the stomach. It's usually dried in the shade to retain its properties.

BARQUILLO
Enoplochiton niger
A type of chiton, this univalve marine mollusk is one of the largest (up to 20 centimeters / 8 inches) and, ecologically, an important grazers that helps control algae on the rocky shores of central Peru. Its preparation is similar to that of abalone.

BATAN
This flat stone tool has been used for grinding since pre-Columbian times. It is used to crush ingredients such as grains or to remove the alkaloid coating from quinoa. The ingredients are crushed on the flat batan with a stone called an uña.

BIJAO
Calathea lutea
Often mistaken for banana leaves, the wide green leaves of the bijao plant are commonly used in Amazonian cuisine. In the juane, the bijao leaf is wrapped around a mixture of rice, chonta (heart of palm), or ground yuca plus spices and other ingredients. Often shaped into containers, the leaves can hold and transport fish, fruits, or other edibles.

BOLDO
Peumus boldus
A small evergreen shrub that can reach 8 m (26 feet) high, boldo grows wild on the coast and in the Andes. Its leaves are used as a sedative and to ease digestion, while the infusion of its bark is used for medicinal purposes, to cure headaches, and insomnia.

BOMBONAJE
Carludovica palmata
A perennial herb in the Cyclanthaceae family, bombanaje grows in tropical humid areas of Central and South America. Fibers from the leaves and stems have been used for centuries to make hats, baskets, and thatched rooftops in rural areas. The soft, white center of the stem-like leaves is used as chonta, a term that traditionally applies to hearts of palm obtained from the aguaje, huasai, or pijuayo palm trees. Bombanaje hearts of palm are less commonly used/known and are more sustainable than other varieties.

BORAGE / BORRAJA
Borago officinalis
An aromatic plant in the Boraginaceae family, borraja (borage in English) has dark green, oval-shaped, hairy leaves, and blue and purple flowers that form clusters on the tips of every branch. The leaves and flowers are used for medicinal purposes in infusions and syrup preparations.

CABUYA
Furcraea andina / Agave americana
These two different species of plant grown in Andean valleys are both referred to as cabuya by Andean communities. Their fiber, obtained by breaking leaves into strips, has been used since pre-Columbian times for making ropes and textiles. The sap from the center of the Agave americana stem, called aguamiel, is collected and then reduced to make a darker dense syrup. This cabuya syrup is produced in central Andean regions, as well as northern coastal ones.

CACAO CRIOLLO
Chocolate made from criollo cacao has a distinctly reddish color, and a complex taste which may include flavors of caramel, nuts, vanilla, and tobacco. As they are less resitant to disease, criollo cacao trees are less common than trinitario and forastero varieties of cacao trees, which produce cacao that dominates the world market. Pure criollo trees are extremely rare, though may be found in parts of Peru.

CACTUS
Opuntia ficus-índica
In this book, the term cactus refers to the tuna plant of the Cactacea family (see page 90), which is widespread in the Andean and coastal valleys of Peru. The fruit, called a "prickly pear" in English, is oval and contains a green, red, or orange pulp that is full of edible black seeds and is high in water content. The thick, spikey green pencas (cactus paddles) contain a viscous gel-like substance.

CAIGUA
Cyclanthera pedata
A domesticated plant species that grows in all regions of Peru, caigua is a climbing annual plant in the Cucurbitaceae family. The fruit is elongated, with a flat base and pointed ends. The vegetable is consumed fresh or cooked, and is believed to have antihypertensive effects.

CAIMITO
Pouteria caimito
A spherical fruit native to the western reaches of the Amazon, caimito grows on trees that are 15 m (50 feet) tall and have elongated leaves. Approximately 9 cm (3 1/2 inches) in diameter, caimito changes from green to yellow or red as it matures. It is known for having a particular latex-like component in its pericarp that makes it gluey when consumed fresh.

CALÉNDULA
(A type of marigold; see AYASISA)

CALLAMPA
Pleurotus / Auricularia polytricha / Drachyopinax spathularia
This is a general term referring to wide, thin-capped mushrooms that grow wild in Andean and Amazonian forests, often on the bark of dead trees. They can be white, yellow, gray, orange, or brown, depending on the species, and can be used raw or cooked.

CAMU CAMU
Myrciaria dubia
This cherry-like fruit of a tree in the Myrtaceae family grows in the very humid, flood-prone Amazonian lowlands. It's round, with a maximum diameter of 4 centimeters (1½ inches) and thin, soft red or purple skin. A whitish-pink to transparent pulp surrounds the seeds and has high acidity. Camu camu contains high amounts of vitamin C and is mainly used in cold beverages or sweets.

CARACHAMA
Pseudorinelepis genibarbis
This is a freshwater fish, in the Loricariidae family (armored catfishes), distributed throughout the Upper Amazon Basin, particularly in cochas (oxbow lakes). It is often grilled whole in market stalls or cooked in caldos (soups).

CASTAÑA
Bertholletia excelsa.
Known in English as the Brazil nut, this Amazonian seed grows on the castaño tree, which can reach up to 30 meters (98 feet) in height. In Peru, it is concentrated in the forests of Madre de Dios and the sustainable activity of collecting castañas is important to the local economy. It's often called Bahuaja nut, because it comes from the area surrounding the Bahuaja Sonene National Park near Puerto Maldonado, an area that is constantly threatened by illegal gold mining and deforestation. Through promoting Bahuaja nut consumption, we hope to instill an awareness of the existence and importance of this park.

CEDRÓN
Aloysia citrodora
Called lemon verbena in English, this flowering herb has a strong scent of lemon and is drunk as an infusion to aid digestion and relieve colds.

CEREBRO DE MAR
Colpomenia sinuosa
Sometimes called sea bubble, this brown marine algae is found in warm to tropical waters of the world's oceans. It contains a phenolic compound called colpol that is used as an antineoplastic agent.

CEVICHE / CEBICHE
This is one of the most emblematic dishes of traditional Peruvian cooking. It is composed mainly of fish or shellfish that are raw or lightly "cooked" by the acidity of a citrus-based mixture called leche de tigre. It is often accompanied by red onions, boiled sweet potato, and choclo (large kernel Andean corn).

CHACO
Hydrous aluminum silicate
This is edible clay collected from pits in the ground, dug especially for consumption in particular areas of the Peruvian Andes and altiplano. After harvesting, the clay is dried in the sun. It is traditionally mixed into a sauce with bitter potatoes to make them harmless to the gastrointestinal system. Ancestral medicine recommends ingestion of a hydrated chaco mixture to prevent gastritis.

CHAMBURU
Carica x heilbornii
This fruit in the Caricaceae family is similar to the common papaya, but smaller. The wild variety is native to tropical forests, but has been domesticated in the Andean and Amazonian regions of Peru. It grows on a small (2 meter / 6 1/2 foot) shrub with large, bright green leaves. The oval-shaped fruit is about 10 centimeters (4 inches) long, yellow or orange, with longitudinal ridges. The pulp is high in water content, creamy, and has many seeds. It is consumed fresh.

CHANCACA
This syrup is made from unrefined sugarcane juice and used as a sauce in traditional sweets, such as picarones (squash fritters).

CHARQUI / CH'ARKI
This is an ancestral technique of preserving meat, usually of llama or alpaca, by covering it in salt and then dehydrating. The process starts by cutting the meat and adding salt (or soaking it in brine for days). The salted pieces of meat are then stacked on top of one another and pressed together periodically (while turning them over from time to time). They are then spread on special trays to air-dry. Finally, the meat is cut into smaller pieces to be stored and consumed within the next several months.

CHERIMOYA
Annona cherimola
The fruit of a small tree which grows in coastal and Andean regions. There is evidence of cultivation in pre-Columbian times and the cherimoya has become one of the most appreciated fruit species in Peru. The skin is green with a soft, scaly texture, and the fruit may be as long as 20 centimeters (8 inches). The pulp is abundant, white, creamy, very sweet, juicy, and aromatic, and can be eaten fresh or used in desserts.

CHIA
Salvia hispanica
This flowering herb in the Lamiaceae family, originally from Central America and southern Mexico, is a domesticated species growing in Andean and high-altitude Amazonian regions in Peru. The seeds are the most valuable part of the plant due to their nutritional benefits. They contain high-quality fiber, proteins, and fatty acids.

CHICHA DE JORA
This is a low-alcohol, fermented maize drink that has been brewed throughout the Andes since pre-Columbian times. Mainly consumed during festivals, it is also used in cooking in many coastal and Andean dishes.

CHINCHO
Tagetes elliptica
A relative of huacatay, this aromatic herb with small yellow flowers grows throughout the Andes. The fresh or dehydrated leaves are commonly used as a condiment for different preparations, usually in soups and stews. Medicinally, it is used as a sedative and digestion aid.

CHIRIC SANANGO
Brunfelsia grandiflora
A native shrub in the Solanaceae (nightshade) family, from the Peruvian Amazon. It has flaky bark and light blue or purple flowers. In Peru, its bark and roots are widely used among local communities for medicinal purposes, usually macerated in aguardiente or used in infusions to cure arthritis and rheumatism, or to heal topical wounds. It is combined with ayahuasca during shamanic rituals.

CHUCHUHUASI / CHUCHUWASHA
Maytenus ebenifolia
The Shawis, a native Amazonian community, register two varieties of this plant in the Celastraceae family: male and female. The male is dark, 15 meters (49 feet) tall, with a thick trunk. The female variety has a thin trunk, a light brown bark, and is only 7–8 meters (23–26 feet) high. The bark is macerated in aguardiente and the result is consumed as an energizer, and used to cure anemia and rheumatism. Additionally, the roots and bark can be cooked overnight and the resulting liquid may be drunk every morning as an energy booster and balance promoter.

CHUÑO
This is an ancient Andean method of preserving potatoes in the high altitudes of the Quechua and Aymara communities. The word is derived from Quechua phonetics and means "potatoes passed from ice to the sun," which explains the steps to make it. This method uses bitter potatoes (*S. juzepczuki* and *S.curtilobum*) and exposes them to the lowest freezing temperatures at night and to the sunlight during the day. Using this method, the potatoes are frozen and then dehydrated. During the day, the farmers step on the potatoes to expel the water content and accelerate the dehydration process. During pre-Columbian times, there were huge storage facilities called colcas, where these chuños could be kept for years to feed the population well beyond the harvest season. White chuño, also called moraya or tunta, is made by soaking the potatoes in pools of water near the riverbank prior to drying them.

CHURO
Pomacea maculata
Large freshwater snail, 5–8 centimeters (2–3 inches) in size, with a thick, spherical, light brown to black shell. Churos inhabit shallow Amazonian rivers and streams with abundant vegetation, mostly at a depth of 10–60 centimeters (4–24 inches) in the clay-rich mud.

CLAVO HUASCA
Tynanthus panurensis
This creeping vine can grow up to 80 meters in length and produces small white flowers that are pollinated by bees and flat, bean-like fruits. The bark and root of the vine have the distinctive smell of cloves and can be macerated in alcohol to help cure colds, though some also claim it to be an aphrodisiac. Clavo huasca is often mixed with or taken after ayahuasca to help settle the stomach during shamanic rituals.

COCA
Erythroxylum coca / Erythroxylum novogranatense
Coca, a bush that grows in Andean and Amazonian regions, is best known for producing light green elliptical leaves, controversial for their use in making cocaine. In Peru and throughout the Andes, the consumption of coca leaves is an important part of Andean culture. Through a custom called chacchado, coca leaves are chewed along with a supplement, sometimes called llipta, made of lime or vegetable ash that helps activate the alkaloids; the resulting substance is held in one side of the mouth and provides energy and strength for those doing strenuous farm work. The custom is considered a social and spiritual cohesion factor in the Andes and not considered taboo within the region. Also, it represents how individuals become adults and take on responsibilities inside their communities. In collective fieldwork, it reinforces solidarity and integration. An infusion made with the coca leaf is very commonly recommended to prevent altitude sickness, but also is presumed to alleviate pain and digestive problems. A sort of flour can be made from the dried leaves as well, used as a thickener for baking.

COCONA
Solanum sessiliflorum
A tart, round Amazonian fruit with uniform yellow skin when mature, as well as creamy, white pulp. Cocona grows on a high shrub (2 meters / 6 1/2 feet) in the Solanaceae family, at altitudes below 1,500 meters (4,920 feet) above sea level. In Peru, twenty-five biotypes have been identified. The fruit is bittersweet and contains high amounts of niacin (vitamin B3). It is mostly used in juices, jams, cocktails, ice creams, and sauces.

CONCHAS NEGRAS
Anadara tuberculosa
This bivalve mollusk, also known as the mangrove cockle, lives buried beneath the mud, amid the roots of mangroves from Laguna Ballena in California to Tumbes on the far north coast of Peru. This black clam has become emblematic of Tumbesino cuisine, particularly the famed ceviche de conchas negras. Its insides and liquid are a deep purple and black with a chewy texture. The combination of overfishing and loss of habitat has resulted in an annual ban on collecting conchas negras in Peru, from mid-February to the end of March.

CONGONA
Peperomia inaequalifolia
An aromatic herb with bright green leaves and rounded edges, congona grows in the humid tropical forests on the mountains in central Andean regions. The leaves are used for infusions and are considered magical by shamans, as a cleansing agent.

COSTEÑO RICE
The term describes rice grown in the coastal valleys of Peru, especially near Lambayeque, where production is the most important. The INIA (National Institute of Agrarian Innovation) has been working on developing mejoradas, varieties that are more resistant and can thrive in Peruvian soil.

CULANTRO
Coriandrum sativum
Not to be confused with culantro in other parts of Latin America, though they are related, culantro in Peru is cilantro (aka fresh coriander). The aromatic herb, brought by the Spanish, has a distinctive flavor and is a key ingredient in many coastal recipes, especially in northern dishes like arroz con pato a la Chiclayana, where it gives the rice its distinctive green color.

CULÉN
Otholobium glandulosum
A wild shrub found in the warmer humid valleys of the central Andes in Peru, Chile, and Bolivia. Culén produces aromatic leaves that are about 2–5 centimeters (3/4–2 inches) long and has small yellow or blue flowers. It has various medicinal uses according to Andean wisdom, including fever relief, antiviral and antibiotic properties, digestion aid, and wound healing.

CUSHURO

Nostoc commune

These green, gelatinous clusters of cyanobacteria globules form in high-altitudes lakes or ponds in the Andes, where they are often seen floating. They vary from 1–10 millimeters (1/16–1/3 inch) in diameter. They are nitrogen fixers and therefore are considered an amino acid precursor with nutritional value. They are typically ingested in hot preparations in Andean communities where they are commonly collected by women and children after rain showers.

DALE DALE

Calathea allouia

This tuber, called the Guinea arrowroot in English, grows in the Peruvian Amazon, as well as tropical areas of South America and the Caribbean where there's humid soil and lots of rain. It is consumed fresh or cooked in stews. Extracts of the leaves are used as a diuretic and energizing tonic.

DONCELLA

Pseudoplatystoma fasciatum

Also called zungaro or the shovel-nosed freshwater catfish, this long-whiskered catfish can weigh as much as 70 kilograms (154 pounds) and is found throughout the Amazon, Corantijn, Essequibo, Orinoco, and Parana River basins.

FLOR DE YUYO

(See YUYO / RED ALGAE)

GAMITANA

Colossoma macropomum

Called tambaqui or pacu in other parts of South America, this freshwater fish is distributed in the Amazon and Orinoco River basins. An omnivore, it feeds on zooplankton, insects, snails, fruits, and decaying plants—essentially anything it finds. It has fatty meat, almost reminiscent of pork, and is most often served grilled.

GUANÁBANA / GRAVIOLA

Annona muricata

The fruit of this 3–10-meter (10–33-foot) tree in the Annonaceae family is called guanábana (or soursop), while the leaves are called graviola. It can be found on the coast and in the Amazon. The ovoid fruit can grow to 40 centimeters (16 inches) in length, has a spiky, green skin, and black seeds that are 2 centimeters (3/4 inch) long. The white, creamy, sweet, and sour pulp can be consumed fresh, in desserts, or in sweetened hot beverages.

GUANACO

Lama guanicoe

This is one of the two wild species of South American camelids (vicuña is the other). It is probably the oldest species in its genre, which also includes the domesticated llama and alpaca. Its range extends from northern Peru to southern Chile and Argentina, particularly arid mountain terrains and desert hills. It has reddish fur with a black face. The particular structure of their feet allows them to wander around the soft sandy terrains of the high Andes while not damaging vegetation or eroding the soil. Guanaco meat has little fat or cholesterol and is often eaten by indigenous communities as charqui or in stews.

HERCAMPURI

Gentianella alborosea

A small perennial herb in the Gentianaceae family with a crooked root and short, dark stem and little violet flowers. It has been used in Andean cultures for centuries to cure liver ailments, as well as to alleviate fevers caused by malaria.

HIERBA LUISA

Cymbopogon citratus

A local form of the lemongrass that grows in Asia, this flowering herb in the Poaceae family is one of the aromatics of many Peruvian gardens. It is often used to flavor dishes with meats or vegetables and may also be drunk in infusions to aid digestion and relieve colds.

HUACATAY

Tagetes minuta

This is a native herb in the Asteraceae family that grows in every region of Peru, including at altitudes as high as 3,800 meters (12,470 feet) above sea level. Its leaves are 12 centimeters (5 inches) long, with six pairs of leaflets, and contain aromatic essential oils. It is used widely in Peruvian cooking in sauces, stews, and soups, and as a condiment in pachamanca, a ritual feast of meats and potatoes cooked by hot stones under the ground. It can also be found as an element in japchi, a sauce made with huacatay, rocoto (chiles), and local cheese. Medicinally, huacatay is used as a digestion aid and for treatment of cardiac palpitations.

HUAMANPINTA

Chuquiraga spinosa

This shrub in the Asteraceae family grows in extreme altitude ecosystems, as well as lower altitudes in the Andes, forming dense groups of plants in rocky forests of the Puna. It has thick stems with hard and spiky orange flowers. It is thought to have the ability to cleanse the blood, and an infusion of the flowers, leaves, and branches is used medicinally as a diuretic.

HUAMANRIPA

Senecio tephrosioides

Growing in the mountains, rocky hills, and altiplano of Peru, tolerating altitudes as high as 4,500 meters (14,760 feet) above sea level, this shrub in the Asteraceae family has small yellow flowers and dark green leaves. Its infusion is used to alleviate flu symptoms, coughs, and other respiratory ailments.

HUAMPO

Heliocarpus americanus

This tree grows both wild and domesticated, from the low jungle up to 3,000 meters (9,840 feet) above sea level. Its bark is used for boats and rope making. Its viscous sap is used in infusions for energy and in sweets.

HUANCAÍNA

This is a thick, traditional sauce with a base of ají amarillo, milk, and Andean cheese (paria or queso fresco). It is commonly served over boiled potatoes and topped with slices of hard-boiled egg and kalamata olives in a dish called papa a la huancaína. The sauce originated in, and is named after, the highland city of Huancayo; huancaína (or huancaíno) is an adjective that means "from Huancayo".

HUARANGO

Prosopis limensis

Similar to algarrobo on the north coast, this tree grows in the desert surrounding Ica, south of Lima. Huarango syrup is thick and dark brown and obtained by boiling the pods to concentrate the sugars. The ecological properties of the genus Prosopis, an integral resource in Peru for at least 5,000 years, have been widely documented to prevent deforestation and promote cultivation.

HUATIA

This temporary, dome-shaped earthen oven made of rocks and dirt is constructed in the fields during the time of a potato harvest in the Andes. After the fire within the oven heats up, the potatoes and other ingredients are placed within just before the oven collapses over them. The food is left buried beneath the hot earth to cook, then is dug out to be served.

HUITO

Genipa americana

The fibrous pulp of this elliptical green fruit that grows on a 30 meter (98-foot) tall Amazonian tree, is consumed fresh or cooked. In Amazonian communities it is fermented with aguardiente and honey in an alcoholic beverage called huitochado. Huito can be processed to obtain a black dye used for fabrics, hair, and skin coloring.

KAÑIWA / CAÑIWA / CAÑIHUA

Chenopodium pallidicaule

This is one of the most important Peruvian pseudocereals (a non-grass used in the same way as a cereal) growing on the altiplano and other Andean regions in Peru. About half the size of quinoa, kañiwa was domesticated about 2,000 years ago and grows between 3,500 and 4,500 meters (11,480 and 14,760 feet) above sea level. The seeds are cooked or roasted and consumed in stews or soups. Sometimes they get pulverized to make cañihuaco (a type of flour that can be used for baking), in drinks like ponche, or in stews and porridges. It is high in protein (essential amino acids) and is thought to be even more nutritionally valuable than quinoa.

KIWICHA

Amaranthus caudatus

A pseudocereal found in the Andes from Colombia to Argentina, kiwicha has been consumed for as long as 4,000 years (seeds have been found in tombs that old). It has been domesticated to grow on the coast, in the Amazon, and as high as 3,500 meters (11,480 feet) above sea level and has different colored seeds, depending on the variety. Seeds are cooked or roasted, sometimes—to make beverages or desserts—with sugar. The leaves are also cooked and added to soups or uchucutas (Andean chile sauces).

LAPA

Fissurella spongiosa

The limpet, a small to medium gastropod mollusk, lives on the rocks of tidal areas along the Peruvian coast. It is most often eaten in ceviche.

LECHE DE TIGRE

Translating to "tiger's milk", this mixture has a strong cultural significance in Peru. Essentially, leche de tigre serves as the base for ceviche. It is most commonly a combination of lime, onion, ají, salt, and the natural juices of the fish. There are dozens of variations of leche de tigres. The lime can be swapped out for another fruit. Various fish and shellfish may be used, or not used at all. Instead of fish, vegetables or mushrooms can even be used. Different ají peppers may be used to adjust the level of spiceiness. How it's adapted and contrasted might be one of the more interesting ways to explore acidity. The experience in balancing each preparation is as important as the ingredients. It should never be too acidic or too bitter.

LECHUGA DE MAR
Ulva lactuca
Sea lettuce, sea grass, lettuce laver, green laver, thin stone brick, or chicory sea lettuce—whatever you call it—this light green marine algae is found floating in mid-intertidal areas in almost every sea. Its habitat is in the sand, on the surface of rocks, and in tidal pools.

LINAZA
Linum usitassimum
Known in English as flax, this plant in the Linaceae family grows in the valleys of Lima and other regions with moist soil and plenty of light exposure. Its seeds are most appreciated for their fiber and oil content (the seeds are 30 to 40 percent oil). When soaked, the seeds' fiber (mucilage) quickly thickens fluids. In Peru, an infusion of these seeds mixed with herbal medicinal plants is used as energizer and aid for digestion.

LOCHE
Cucurbita moschata
In Peru, this squash is grown along the northern coast (Lambayeque) and in the high Amazon. It was one of the first domesticated species in the Zaña Valley between 6,000 and 8,000 years ago and is linked directly to the Mochica culture. The shape is variable, though it normally is elongated with a wide, round base. It has dark green skin and bright orange and yellow pulp. The flesh, pulp, and seeds are consumed unripe or mature in various preparations, which include purées, sweets, and numerous emblematic dishes of the north coast. The flowers can be filled and deep-fried, and the sprouts are used fresh in salads.

LOMO SALTADO
This is a traditional Peruvian dish that showcases the influence of Chinese immigration on Peruvian food. It consists of cooking small pieces of beef in a wok with onions, tomatoes, and ají chile. It is usually accompanied by fried potatoes and cilantro.

LÚCUMA
Pouteria lucuma
Cultivated since pre-Columbian times, lúcuma grows at altitudes as high as 3,000 meters (9,840 feet) above sea level, and on the coast, and in the Amazon. The Lucumo valleys are 45 minutes south of Lima. The fruit, which is in the Sapotaceae family, is round with a dark-green brownish skin and intense, dry yellow or orange pulp with one or two large, shiny brown seeds. It is consumed fresh, ground into a powder, and also used in desserts, especially in ice creams. It is sweet, starchy, and creamy and has a flavor reminiscent of a cross between pumpkin and maple syrup.

MACA
Lepidium meyenii
This is one of the first roots consumed during pre-Incan times in Peru. During the first year of the plant's growth, the roots and stems are developed, and in the second, the flowers and fruit. In Peru, maca grows throughout the central Andes and resists very low temperature and harsh conditions. It has a conical, radish-like shape, and is light yellow or orange, with a soft surface. Often called Peruvian ginseng, it's considered to be an energy booster and is presumed to be an aphrodisiac.

MACAMBO
Theobroma bicolor
A mostly wild relative of cacao, macambo is found growing in low and high jungle environments up to 1,000 meters (3,280 feet) above sea level, from Mexico to the Amazon. The fruit is elliptical and large, sometimes weighing as much as 3 kilograms (6 1/2 pounds). The skin turns from green to yellow when mature. In indigenous Amazonian recipes the seeds are often roasted, cooked in stews, or fried. The pulp is also edible and is used in beverages.

MAÍZ MORADO
Zea mays
Growing in the Andes and along the coast of Peru, this intensely purple corn is used in several traditional Peruvian recipes, such as chicha morada (a sort of purple corn juice) and mazamorra morada (purple corn pudding). Kernels of this purple corn are soaked in water to attain a deep purple color that can be used as a dye.

MALVA
Malachra ruderalis
These flowers found in the Amazon and highlands are light blue and violet, and when dehydrated they maintain the same color for a long time and dye the water blue. An infusion of the roots is thought to cure the common cold, while a juice made from the leaves has anti-inflammatory properties. The flowers are used in an infusion with the leaves to treat irritated eyes.

MANAYUPA
Desmodium mollicum
A wild herbal plant growing in Andean valleys between 1,000 and 3,200 meters (3,280 and 10,500 feet) above sea level, manayupa is used in local communities as a cleansing agent and allergy reliever. The leaves are typically infused in hot water, then the liquid is consumed.

MARACUYÁ
Passiflora edulis
This round yellow fruit is from a climbing plant, commonly known as passionfruit, cultivated mostly in the Amazonian and Andean regions. The interior is an intense orange or yellow, mucilaginous pulp that is very acidic and full of small black seeds. It is used mostly in sweet preparations like beverages, sauces, or sorbets.

MARKHU / MARKHO / MARKO / MARCO
Ambrosia peruviana
In the rocky mountains of the Andes at altitudes higher than 3,500 meters (11,480 feet) above sea level, this shrub in the Asteraceae family has aromatic leaves and green or yellow flowers. Infusions of the leaves are thought to have antirheumatic abilities and cure digestive issues.

MARAÑON
Anacardium occidentale
In Peru, the cashew fruit grows in tropical forests of the Amazon, as well as on the far northern coast. The fruit is red-orange, pear-shaped, and about 8 centimeters (3 inches) long. It is consumed fresh or in juices and jams. The kidney-shaped, greenish seed (the "nut"), which hangs from the bottom of the cashew fruit, can be roasted, processed into oil, or used as a thickener in soups or stews.

MASHUA / MASHWA
Tropaeolum tuberosum
A tuber that grows throughout the Andes from Colombia to Argentina, mashua has been cultivated in Peru since pre-Columbian times and has been represented on the ceramics of various ancient cultures. It grows wild at altitudes higher than 3,000 meters (9,840 feet) above sea level and more than 100 varieties of mashuas have been identified in the Andes. The tuber has a conical shape and may be yellow, greenish, purple, or red. Mashuas are usually exposed to sunlight for several days after harvest before consumption to turn starches into sugars, producing a sweeter flavor. Medicinally, they are used as an antibiotic or to treat kidney stones.

MATICO
Piper aduncum
Native to South America, the matico plant's long, dark green aromatic leaves have a spicy taste and smell. A paste is made with the crushed leaves and can be used to heal wounds. It can also be used as an anti-ulcerative agent by making an infusion, leaving it to rest for an hour, and then ingesting it over the following several days.

MIEL DE PALO
This very particular honey is produced on the north coast of Peru, in the Piura and Tumbes regions, in the hills of the dry forest. Meliponas (stingless bees) build their hives in holes of endemic Prosopis trees like the algarrobo. There is an interesting relationship between the termites that feed from the bark of these trees and the bees that seek out and use the termite holes. The resulting honey is thick and golden brown, sweet and tangy, and has been collected for centuries by locals. It is thought to cure inflammatory diseases and alleviate respiratory symptoms.

MOLLE
Schinus molle
The tiny, reddish-pink spherical fruits of this evergreen tree have a strong aroma and are similar to black peppercorns when dried. The Inca used the sweeter outer part of the ripe fruit to make a drink and syrup.

MORAYA
(A Quechua word that refers to the white chuño; see CHUÑO)

MUCÍLAGO DE CACAO
Theobroma cacao
This is the mucilage that covers cacao seeds, just under the pulp. This fluid comes out easily during the cacao bean fermentation process. Sweet and white / pink liquid, with a low density, it has been consumed fresh by local communities and also used for jams.

MULLACA
Muehlenbeckia volcanica
A creeping plant in the Polygonaceae family that grows in rocky parts of the Andes, mullaca must be harvested by digging deep to extract its roots. Its leaves and branches are used in infusions to treat fevers and coughs, while the roots can help soothe asthma and bronchitis.

MUÑA
Minthostachys mollis / Minthostachys setosa / Minthostachys tormentosa
This aromatic plant in the Lamiaceae (aka mint) family usually grows wild at high altitudes (more than 2,200 meters / 7,220 feet) above sea level in light soils with slightly alkaline sand and clay. It has aromatic green leaves that are consumed in infusions, soups, and stews. Medicinally, it is mainly used as an antibacterial for infections in the digestive system. The essential oils are present more intensely in the tormentosa species.

OCA
Oxalis tuberosa
Cultivated in the Andes between 3,000 and 4,000 meters (9,840 and 13,120 feet) above sea level, oca plays an important role in crop rotation. Hardy and frost resistant, the plant's long, cylindrical tubers range in color from white to grayish purple. It has a sharp taste when eaten raw, though exposure to sunlight after harvest, turning starches into sugars, gives oca a sweeter flavor. Oca can be baked, roasted, or cooked in stews. The stems can be used much like rhubarb, while leaves and young shoots can be eaten fresh.

OLLUCO / ULLUKU / PAPALISA
Ullucus tuberosus
Growing in a range of colors and shapes, olluco is a widely cultivated crop in the Andes that produces the second most common tuber in Peru after the potato. This tuber has a crisp texture, high water content, and sweet flavor. When cooked, it stays firm with a slight crunch, therefore it is a good candidate for boiling or pickling. In Peru, it is most commonly used in the dish olluquito con charqui, where it is finely diced and added to a stew made with dehydrated meat (traditionally llama or alpaca). The leaves are rich in calcium, carotenes, and protein and can be eaten fresh, having a texture similar to spinach.

PACAE
Inga feuillei
Native to Andean valleys, pacae trees have nitrogen-fixing roots and are often used for shade. They produce long green pods filled with seeds surrounded by an edible white cotton candy-like pulp.

PAICHE
Arapaima gigas
Among the world's largest freshwater fish, paiche, also called arapaima or pirarucu in other parts of the Amazon River basin outside of Peru, can grow as long as 3 meters (10 feet) in length and weigh as much as 200 kilograms (440 pounds). An air breather, it rises to the surface of the water. It has colorful, blackish green and red scales that have a mineralized hard outer layer. While paiche is endangered in parts of the Amazon due to overfishing, sustainable projects throughout the region, including farm-raised paiche, have been rather successful and the fish is available for export. It has a high protein content and lower fat percentage than other white-fleshed fish species, with a flavor similar to Chilean sea bass. It is typically grilled, pan-seared, or smoked. Its high levels of collagen, let it develop a nice crust when cooked. Indigenous communities in the Amazon usually salt and sun-dry paiche flesh, which can be taken into the forest during hunting expeditions, used in various hot preparations, or rolled up to be sold in markets.

PAICO
Dysphania ambrosioides
An aromatic herb, called epazote in Mexico, which can grow at nearly any altitude, paico has been used since pre-Columbian times in Peru. It is eaten as a leaf vegetable or used to season chupes (chowders) and caldos (soups), as well as pachamanca (a ritual feast cooked in an earthen oven).

PALLAR
Phaseolus lunatus
Better known as butter beans or lima beans in English, the pallar was domesticated in the Andes around 4,000 years ago. A favorite crop of the Moche civilization on the north coast, it was featured prominently in their art and ceramics.

PANELA
This unrefined whole cane sugar, made from boiled and evaporated sugarcane juice, has been used throughout Latin America for centuries. Often sold in bricks, in Peru bags of panela come in granulated form, like table sugar.

PAPA
Solanum tuberosum
Peru's most important contribution to the culinary world, the potato is the world's fourth largest food crop and thousands of varieties grow in Peru. One of the most common is the papa amarilla (yellow potato), with a soft, crumbly texture. Regional variations of papas nativas, the majority of which are still wild, come in an array of shapes and colors, including red blue, purple, and black.

PAPA VOLADORA / SACHAPAPA
Dioscorea trifida
The papa voladora, or flying potato, is a waxy yam that grows suspended in the air like a piece of fruit. It grows in a variety of shapes and colors, including white, purple, and black.

PATA DE GALLO
Lessonia nigrescens
This is a species of kelp native to the southern Pacific Ocean. It is harvested commercially for alginate, a viscous gum used as a thickening and gelling agent in the food industry.

PEPINO MELÓN
Solanum muricatum
Native to the Andes and grown in coastal valleys, this sweet fruit has a flavor that is a cross between melon and cucumber (pepino)—hence the name.

POMARROSA
Syzygium jambos
Sometimes called the rose apple, despite being neither a rose nor an apple, the pomarrosa has a deep red skin and whitish flesh. It grows at humid, low to medium altitudes of Peru. The fruit bruises easily and only lasts for a few days once picked. They are usually eaten fresh or cooked into jams.

QUEBRANTA
Peru's only indigenous vinifera variety, Quebranta was the result of the cross of mollar and negra criolla (país or negra peruana) grapes, which were brought by the Spanish, sometime in the sixteenth century. The non-aromatic Quebranta is one of the primary grapes used for making pisco.

QUEÑUAL
Polylepis incana / Polylepis racemosa
With a typically crooked trunk and abundant branches, this native Andean tree is best identified by the copper bark and paper-like membranous sheets constantly peeling off the branches and trunk. Queñuales trees are typically found between 2,800 and 5,000 meters (9,190 and 16,400 feet) above sea level and can resist very low temperatures and extreme altitudes, as well as the variability of soil conditions. In Andean communities, an infusion of the bark and leaves is thought to cure respiratory symptoms and rheumatism. The trees are considered building blocks of high Andean ecosystems, as they store significant amounts of water and help prevent soil erosion. However, over the last several centuries, the queñuales have been gradually replaced by faster-growing eucalyptus trees.

QUINOA
Chenopodium quinoa
One of the most important Andean grain crops produced in the Andes and

altiplano of Peru and Bolivia, quinoa was domesticated between 3,000 and 4,000 years ago in the area around Lake Titicaca. It can grow anywhere from the coast to over 4,000 meters (13,120 feet) above sea level, though most production falls somewhere between 2,500 and 4,000 meters (8,300 and 13,120 feet) above sea level. Technically a seed, this pseudocereal is high in protein and essential amino acids and comes in a rainbow of colors—white, pink, red, and black. Cooked in a fashion similar to rice, quinoa has a delicate, nutty flavor and is used in a range of dishes, including salads, porridges, and side dishes. It can be processed into a flour, which can be used for baking. The leaves and flower heads are edible and nutritious, too.

RED OXALIS
Oxalis corniculata
Growing like weeds in urban gardens such the one at Central, red oxalis, aka wood sorrel has trifoliate leaves with heart shaped leaflets, plus tiny bright yellow flowers and capsuled fruit. The leaves and flowers are edible and have a lemony taste.

RETAMA
Cassia reticulata
According to Andean folklore, bright yellow retama flowers represent a bright side to sadness and sorrow, a reason to smile and be happy. The leaves of this 5 meter (16-foot) high shrub, which grows near lakes and rivers in humid areas in the central Andes or Amazon jungle, are used as an insect repellent. An infusion of the flowers is thought to protect the liver and cure gastric spasms, as well as treat hypertension. For skin conditions, locals immerse retama petals in their bath water.

ROCOTO
Capsicum pubescens
With a Scoville score of 12,000–50,000 units, the rocoto chile is one of the hottest in Peru. It is typically grown in Andean regions and has been cultivated for about 2,000 years in the region. Slightly smaller than a bell pepper, it has a red and/or orange skin when mature. Traditional in Andean cooking, rocoto is used dried as a condiment, in sauces and dressings, and also as a colorant. Rocoto chiles are emblematic of Arequipeña cuisine and are the signature ingredient of that region's iconic dish, rocoto relleno (stuffed rocoto peppers).

RUDA
Ruta graveolens
These are the aromatic leaves of a 1 meter (3.3 foot) tall species of a shrub in the Rutaceae family cultivated in valleys and high-altitude mountains in the Andes. The stem is woody and rigid, the leaves blue-green (pale on the reverse face), and oval-shaped. Ruda's aromatic leaves are used to heal migraines, malaria, fevers, and to rid one of parasites.

SACHA AJO
Mansoa alliacea
A wild, tropical shrub native to the Amazon, with leaves that have a strong smell and flavor similar to garlic. The leaves are used as a condiment or in tea, which is thought to cure colds. Some indigenous groups prepare the roots in a sugarcane alcohol tincture to make a body tonic.

SACHA CULANTRO / JUNGLE CULANTRO / FALSE CULANTRO
Eryngium foetidum
Sacha culantro has small, pointy leaves and a strong culantro-like flavor. It is used much like culantro, as a condiment and in sauces.

SACHA INCHI
Plukenetia volubilis
Sometimes called the Inca peanut, sacha inchi has been cultivated in the Amazon for centuries. The plant produces a green fruit that ripens blackish brown and contains a seed within each of its four or five lobes. High in protein and oil content, the seeds are inedible raw, but can be roasted as a snack or made into oil. Sacha inchi seeds have a mild, nutty flavor.

SANGRE DE GRADO
Croton lechleri
Sangre de grado is a flowering plant native to the northwestern part of South America. It is known for producing a thick red latex-like resin used as a dye. Indigenous populations apply it directly to wounds.

SALICORNIA
Salicornia fruticosa
A type of succulent, growing mostly on beaches and coastal areas, salicornia is also known as sea bean, sea asparagus, samphire, or glasswort in other parts of the world. Edible raw or cooked, salicornia has the flavor of young asparagus or spinach stems with a touch of salt.

SANDIA COFFEE
This premium Peruvian coffee is produced by Quechua and Aymara farmers in the Valle de Sandia, within the region of Puno.

SAPOTE
Pouteria sapota
This is a fruit tree found throughout Central and South America. Sapote has a brown skin and soft, creamy orange or red flesh. Its flavor has notes of sweet potato, honey, apricot, or almond, and it can be eaten raw, or in jams and desserts.

SARGAZO / SARGASSUM
Macrocystis pyrifera
This robust species of kelp thick leaves and delicate stems. It is found around the Pacific Rim and can grow as large as 45 meters (145 feet) long in dense stands called kelp forests, which provide food and shelter for countless marine animals. Rich in iodine and potassium, sargazo is an underutilized food source and can be prepared much like most other sea vegetables.

SAÚCO
Sambucus nigra subsp. peruviana
One of the few species of elderberries that can be eaten uncooked, sauco is native to the Andes and is used in jams, sauces, and syrups. The dark purple berry has a bittersweet taste.

SHIMBILLO
Inga edulis
From the same family as pacae, this 8 meter (26-foot) tall tree has a fruit that is contained in pods with the nickname the "ice cream bean" because of its sweet flavor and smooth texture. The tree's bark is used by indigenous Amazonians for its medicinal properties.

STEVIA
Stevia rebaudiana
Originally from Paraguay and used by the Guaraní to sweeten mate or to chew the sweet leaves, stevia thrives in the humid, tropical environments of Peru like the Amazon and high jungle. The leaves are primarily used as a sweetener, but also eaten fresh, in tea, or as syrup.

TAMARILLO / TOMATE DE ÁRBOL / SACHATOMATE
Solanum betaceum
Native to the subtropical Andes and cultivated in subtropical or warm temperate regions, this tree tomato has various types distinguished by their skin colors: solid deep purple, blood red, orange, yellow, or red-and-yellow. They may have faint dark, longitudinal stripes. The ripe fruit is ovoid in shape and smooth-skinned and contains many small seeds. It has a slightly sour and astringent taste with a delicate and characteristic aroma. Tamarillo is mostly consumed fresh or in various

preparations such as salads, sauces, soups, compotes, ice creams, juices, and liqueurs.

TARA
Caesalpinia spinosa
Growing in dry forests from 0 to 4,500 meters (14,760 feet) above sea level, this leguminous tree produces a fruit high in tannins, which are extracted after a simple boiling process. A yellow to gray coloring is obtained from the pods and is used for dyeing fabric. In culinary preparations it is used as a thickening agent and stabilizer.

TARWI
Lupinus mutabilis
This is a species of lupin that has grown in the Andes at 800–3,000 meters (2,625–9,840 feet) above sea level for over 1,500 years. Tarwi is highly effective in fixing nitrogen from the air, replenishing the health of the soil. High in protein and fat, the white seed is a staple of traditional Andean diets, often boiled and added to stews and salads. The seeds have a bitter taste when raw because of their high alkaloid content, which can be remedied by soaking them in water for a few days.

TIN TIN
Passiflora pinnatistipula
A passion flower that grows in the Andes above 2,500 meters (8,200 feet) above sea level, tin tín produces a yellow, oblong fruit with a sweet, orange–like pulp that is used in drinks and jams.

TIRADITO
A traditional dish in cevicherias, tiradito is similar to ceviche but without the onions and with a different cut to the fish. It was introduced to Peruvian cuisine by Japanese chefs in Lima and consists of sliced raw fish barely doused in leche de tigre (a lime–based liquid) and sometimes an ají chile cream. The thickness of the cut of the fish is somewhere between carpaccio and sashimi.

TOCOSH
A traditional Quechua food made by fermenting and dehydrating tubers since the Chavín culture. The papa canchan or papa rosada, a potato with a thin, pink skin, and mild flavor is commonly used, though other varieties of potatoes, oca, or mashua can also be used. The Tocosh has a notoriously sharp odor and flavor. It's used in stews or to make mazamorra de tocosh, a porridge prepared by boiling tocosh with water, sugar, cinnamon, and cloves. As penicillin is produced during the fermentation process, tocosh

has been considered a natural antibiotic, as well as a remedy for stomach ulcers, gastritis, digestion, and respiratory illnesses.

TUCUNARÉ / PACA
Cichla temensis
Known in English as the speckled peacock bass, this feisty game fish can weigh as much as 12 kilograms (26 pounds) and inhabits the Amazon and Orinoco River basins. Tucunaré has a firm white flesh with a mild flavor and not a lot of bones. It's often grilled, baked, or added to stews.

TUMBO
Passiflora tripartita
Sometimes called the banana passion fruit, the oblong–shaped tumbo is native to the Andes. It has a bittersweet, slightly sour pulp, and the fruits that grow in the warmer, tropical areas tend to be larger and sweeter. Spanish conquistadors encountered coastal civilizations mixing tumbo pulp with raw fish, a crude form of ceviche. The pulp is often used in juices, cocktails, and desserts.

TUNA
Opuntia ficus-indica
This cactus fruit, or prickly pear, has a pink or green skin and a bright pink pulp (which can be used as a dye) with black seeds. It has been cultivated since pre–Colombian times and can be eaten raw or in juices or jams.

TUNTA
Developed in the Andean highlands between 2,000 and 3,000 years ago, this method of potato preservation is done by a natural lyophilization, or freeze–drying, process. The smell is intense, though familiar to Andean communities and not to be diluted. Tunta is rehydrated in stews and hot preparations, and is commonly served on its own with a slice of fresh cheese. Tunta produced on the altiplano, particularly near Lake Titicaca outside of Puno, is of particularly high quality.

UCHUCUTA
In Quechua, uchu means ají (chile) and cuta means minced or ground. It is a common name for chile sauces in the Andes, though recipes may vary considerably.

UÑA DE GATO
Uncaria tomentosa
This is an Amazonian vine known as the cat's claw because of hook–like thorns that grow on it. The vines can reach more than 30 meters (98 feet) high into the rainforest canopy. The

roots and inner bark are renowned for their alleged anti–inflammatory, immunostimulant, antioxidant, and anticancer properties.

UNGURAHUI
Oenocarpus bataua
A large, erect palm tree native to the Amazonian rainforest, Amazonian uplands, and flood plains, ungurahui bears an edible fruit that is rich in protein and oil. Resembling a large black olive, the fruit is often mixed with sugar and served as a juice or made into ice cream.

YACÓN
Smallanthus sonchifolius
This perennial Andean plant produces a crisp, sweet–tasting edible root that is rich in fruit sugars and grows in clusters of four to twenty roots. A relative of the Jerusalem artichoke, it has a texture and flavor similar to jicama. Yacón has a high water content and is versatile: It can be eaten raw, in juices, or made into a syrup.

YUCA
Manihot esculenta
Also known as cassava or manioc, yuca is a staple crop of the Amazon and one of the largest sources of carbohydrates in Latin America and the Caribbean. The high–yield plant is drought-tolerant and can grow on marginal soils, making it a reliable crop throughout the region. The tall, semiwoody, perennial shrub has a tuberous edible root, which grows in clusters of four to eight at the base. As it contains toxic properties, particularly the more bitter varieties, yuca must undergo some form of cooking, fermentation, or soaking before it is eaten. In Peru there are dozens of different preparations for yuca. It can be boiled, baked, steamed, grilled, or fried. It is often added to stews and boiled pieces are sometimes set in a bowl of ceviche. It can also be ground into flour, which can then be used to bake bread. Yuca can be fermented and reduced to make ají negro, a rich, spicy paste used in some traditional Amazonian villages.

YUYO / RED ALGAE
Chondracanthus chamissoi
Endemic to cold waters of the Humboldt Current along the southern Pacific coast of South America (from Paita, Peru to Chiloe, Chile), this is one of the region's most abundant red algae. It is often a garnish in a bowl of ceviche or other seafood preparations in Peru.

ZÚNGARO
(see DONCELLA)

INDEX

A
abuta 242
achiote *see* **annatto**
aguaje 242
aguardiente 242
    barks (for maceration) *180*, 181
aguaymanto (cape gooseberry) 242
airampo 242
    airampo dye 90, *91*
    red Amazon 176, *177*
ají amarillo 242
    avocado & seeds 84, *85*
    diversity of maize 68, *69*
ají charapita 242
ají limo 242
    tiger's milk 30
ají panca 242
    heart 118, *119*
ajosquiro 242
algae
    avocado & seeds 84, *85*
    carachama y yacón 194, *195*
    cerebro de mar 243
    fish of high-altitude waters 158, *159*
    lechuga de mar 246
    harvest & gathering 36, *37*
    octopus in its coral 31, *32, 33*
    pata de gallo 247
    sargazo 248
    scallop fossil 60, *61*
    shells in the desert 72, *73*
    spiders of the rock 28, *29*
    tree & sweet algae 78, *79*
    yuyo 249
algarrobo 242
alpaca & amaranth 134, *135*
alpaca y kiwicha 134, *135*
altiplano (3,900 m / 12,795 ft) 140–142
    altiplano clay [recipe] 151, *152*
    cacao crystals 240
    diversity of quinoas 144, *145*
    fish of high-altitude waters 158, *159*
    ichu [recipe] 148, *149*
    llama & chlorophyll *145*, 146
    pseudocereals [recipe] 154, *155*
    tunta thickener 150
altura extrema (4,200 m / 13,780 ft) 122–124
    alpaca & amaranth 134, *135*
    Andean corn 130, *131*
    gathering of cushuro 136, *137*
    tin tin [recipe] 132, *133*
    tocosh [recipe] 126, *127*
amaranth *see* **kiwicha**
amarillo de tubérculos 86, *87*
Amazonía (230 m / 755 ft) 188–190
    blood of the tree 196, *197*
    carachama & yacón 194, *195*
    fish of the red seeds, the 192, *193*
    gamitana [recipe] 198, *199*
    huito dye 210, *211*
    rose apple [recipe] 202, *203*
    tucunaré [recipe] 206, *207*
    ungurahui dye 204, *205*
Amazonía roja 176, *177*
anchoveta 242
Andean corn 130, *131*
Andes (3,600 m / 11,811 ft) 98–99

extreme stems *104*, 105
fermentation in the Andes 128, *129*
heart 118, *119*
ocas & ollucos in Maras 102, *103*
pork in mashuas 112, *113*
queñual paper 108, *109*
sweet mashua 114, 115
yacón crystals 239
annatto / achiote 242
    fish of the red seeds, the 192, *193*
    flying potato 228, *229*
    alpaca & amaranth 134, *135*
    avocado & seeds 84, *85*
arañas de roca 28, *29*
arbol y alga dulce 78, *79*
arcilla de altiplano 151, *152*
arracacha 242
    yellow tubers 86, *87*
atadijo 242
avocado & seeds 84, *85*
ayahuasca 242
ayasisa 242

B
Bahuaja nut oil
    fish of the red seeds, the 192, *193*
    flying potato 228, *229*
    fruits, seeds & chocolate 230, *231*
    tucunaré [recipe] 206, *207*
Bahuaja nuts / castaña 243
    tucunaré [recipe] 206, *207*
bajo andino (1,600 m / 5,249 ft) 82–83
    airampo dye 90, *91*
    avocado & seeds 84, *85*
    leaves of the Andean Valley 88, *89*
    lúcuma, cactus & retama 92, *93*
    yellow tubers 86, *87*
bananas
    fruits, seeds & chocolate 230, *231*
barks (for maceration) *180*, 181
barquillos (chiton) 242
    stone tongue 48, *49*
batan 242
beef heart
    heart 118, *119*
    pseudocereals [recipe] 154, *155*
beef short ribs
    pseudocereals [recipe] 154, *155*
beets / beetroot
    avocado & seeds 84, *85*
beverages
    aguardiente 242
    chicha de jora 243
    solar infusion of purple corn 76, *77*
bijao 242
boldo 243
bombonaje 243
    bombonaje [recipe] *170*, 171
    gamitana [recipe] 198, *199*
borraja (borage) 243
    mangrove soil 50, *51*
Brazil nuts *see* **Bahuaja nuts**
butter beans *see* **pallar**

C
cabuya 243
cacao 214–216
    cacao criollo 243

cacao crystals 240
    fruits, seeds & chocolate 230, *231*
    macambo 246
    mucílago de cacao 247
    ollucos & cacao 178, *179*
    sapote, ungurahui & macambo 218, *219*
    wood & cacao 232, *233*
cacao crystals 240
    altiplano clay [recipe] 151, *152*
    huampo gel 164, *165*
    ollucos & cacao 178, *179*
    sapote, ungurahui & macambo 218, *219*
cactus 243
    cactus gel 74, *75*
    lúcuma, cactus & retama 92, *93*
    rose apple [recipe] 202, *203*
    shells in the desert 72, *73*
    tuna (cactus) 249
caigua 243
    shells in the desert 72, *73*
caimito 243
callampa 243
camu camu 243
cape gooseberry *see* **aguaymanto**
carachama y yacón 194, *195*
carachama 243
    carachama & yacón 194, *195*
cascarilla bark (for macerations) 181
cashew *see* **marañon**
cassava *see also* **tapioca flour; yuca**
    cassava starch 64, *65*
castaña (Bahuaja nut / Brazil nut) 243
    tucunaré [recipe] 206, *207*
catahua bark (for macerations) 181
cedrón (lemon verbena) 243
    huampo gelatin 172, *173*
    leaves of the Andean Valley 88, *89*
    sweet mashua 114, *115*
cerdo en mashuas 112, *113*
cerebro de mar (sea bubble) 243
    octopus in its coral 31, *32*
ceviche / cebiche 243
chaco 243
    altiplano clay [recipe] 151, *152*
    extreme stems *104*, 105
    gathering of cushuro 136, *137*
    ocas and ollucos in Maras 102, *103*
chamburu 243
    leaves of the Andean Valley 88, *89*
chancaca 243
    spiders of the rock 28, *29*
chancayano amarillo corn
    diversity of maize 68, *69*
chaparreño corn
    diversity of maize 68, *69*
charqui / ch'arki 243
Chazuta (260 m / 853 ft) 214–216
    flying potato 228, *229*
    fruits, seeds & chocolate 230, *231*
    honey in the jungle 222, *223*
    sapote, ungurahui & macambo 218, *219*
    wood & cacao 232, *233*
    yacón root & duck 226, *227*
cherimoya 244
chía 243

blood of the tree 196, 197
  fruits, seeds & chocolate 230, 231
  leaves of the Andean Valley 88, 89

chicha de jora 243
  heart 118, 119
chile peppers
  ají amarillo 242
  ají charapita 242
  ají limo 242
  ají panca 242
  rocoto 248
chincho 243
  bombonaje 170, 171
  gathering of cushuro 136, 137
  heart 118, 119
  leaves of the Andean Valley 88, 89
  pseudocereals [recipe] 154, 155
  tin tin [recipe] 132, 133
  yellow tubers 86, 87
chiric sanango 244
chiton see **barguillo**
choclos andinos 130, 131
chocolate see also **cacao**
  altiplano clay [recipe] 151, 152
  fruits, seeds & chocolate 230, 231
chuchuhuasi / chuchuwasha 244
  bark (for macerations) 181
  wood & cacao 232, 233
chuño 244
  tin tin [recipe] 132, 133
churos 244
  blood of the tree 196, 197
cilantro (coriander) 244
  diversity of maize 68, 69
  gathering of cushuro 136, 137
  spiders of the rock 28, 29
  tiger's milk 30
clams
  harvest & gathering 36, 37
  mangrove soil 50, 51
  rock of the mangroves 52, 53
clavo huasca 244
clay, edible see **chaco**
coca 244
  coca dough 166, 167
  fish of high-altitude waters 158, 159
cochayuyo see **yuyo**
cocona 244
  honey in the jungle 222, 223
coffee
  altiplano clay [recipe] 151, 152
  Sandia coffee 248
color de airampo 90, 91
color de huito 210, 211
color de ungurahui 204, 205
conchas del desierto 72, 73
conchas negras 244
  rock of the mangroves 52, 53
congona 244
corazón 118, 119
coriander see **cilantro**
corn
  Andean corn 130, 131
  diversity of maize 68, 69
  maíz morado 246
  solar infusion of purple corn 76, 77
cortezas 180, 181

coruca corn
  diversity of maize 68, 69
cosecha y recolección 36, 37
costeño rice 244
  octopus in its coral 31, 32
crab
  spiders of the rock 28, 29
cristales de cacao 240
cristales de huarango 235
cristales de pacae 234
cristales de stevia 238
cristales de yacón 239
crystals (sweeteners)
  cacao crystals 240
  huarango crystals 235
  pacae crystals 234
  stevia crystals 238
  yacón crystals 239
culén 244
cushuro 98, 245
  gathering of cushuro 136, 137
  llama & chlorophyll 146, 147

D
dale dale 245
  huampo gelatin 172, 173
diversidad de maíz 68, 69
diversidad de quinuas 144, 145
diversity of maize 68, 69
diversity of quinoas 144, 145
doncella / zúngaro 245
  blood of the tree 196, 197
drinks see **beverages**
duck, yacón root & 226, 227
dulce mashua 114, 115
dyes
  airampo dye 90, 91
  huito dye 210, 211
  ungurahui dye 204, 205

E
el ichu 148, 149
el pez de las semillas rojas 192, 193
epazote see **paico**
Escalera (800 m / 2,625 ft) 162–163
  barks [recipe] 180, 181
  bombonaje [recipe] 170, 171
  coca dough 166, 167
  huampo gel 164, 165
  huampo gelatin 172, 173
  ollucos & cacao 178, 179
  red Amazon 176, 177
  sanación 184, 185
espesante de tunta, 150
extreme stems 104, 105

F
fermentación en los Andes 128, 129
fish
  anchoveta 242
  carachama 243
  carachama & yacón 194, 195
  doncella 245
  fish of high-altitude waters 158, 159
  fish of the red seeds, the 192, 193
  gamitana 245
  gamitana [recipe] 198, 199
  paiche 247

  red Amazon 176, 177
  tucunaré 249
  tucunaré [recipe] 206, 207
flax see **linaza**
flying potato 228, 229
fósil de concha 60, 61
fruit
  aguaymanto 242
  airampo 242
  caimito 243
  camu camu 243
  chamburu 243
  cherimoya 244
  cocona 244
  guanábana 245
  huito 189, 245
  lúcuma 246
  maracuyá 246
  pepino melón 247
  pomarrosa 247
  quebranta 247
  sapote 248
  saúco 248
  tin tin 249
  tomate de árbol 248
  tumbo 249
  fruits, seeds & chocolate 230, 231
frutas, semillas y chocolate 230, 231

G
gamitana 245
  fish of the red seeds, the 192, 193
  gamitana [recipe] 198, 199
  gathering of cushuro 136, 137
gel de cactus 74, 75
gel de huampo 164, 165
gelatin, huampo 172, 173
gelatina de huampo 172, 173
gels
  cactus gel 74, 75
  huampo gel 164, 165
grapes
  quebranta 247
guanábana (soursop) / graviola 245
  honey in the jungle 222, 223
guanaco 245
Guinea arrowroot see **dale dale**

H
harvest & gathering 36, 37
herbs
  bombonaje 243
  borraja 243
  cedrón 243
  chincho 243
  congona 244
  culantro 244
  hercampuri 245
  hierba luisa 245
  huacatay 245
  muña 247
  paico 247
hercampuri 245
  lúcuma, cactus & retama 92, 93
hierba buena
  fruits, seeds & chocolate 230, 231
  leaves of the Andean Valley 88, 89
  yacón root & duck 226, 227

hierba luisa (lemongrass) 245
  rose apple [recipe] 202, 203
high plains see **altiplanto**
hojas de valle andino 88, 89
honey
  honey in the jungle 222, 223
  miel de palo 247
huacatay 245
  huampo gelatin 172, 173
  leaves of the Andean Valley 88, 89
  lúcuma, cactus & retama 92, 93
  pseudocereals [recipe] 154, 155
  red Amazon 176, 177
  tin tin [recipe] 132, 133
  yellow tubers 86, 87
huamanpinta 245
huamanripa 245
  heart 118, 119
  leaves of the Andean Valley 88, 89
huampo 172, 245
  honey in the jungle 222, 223
  huampo gel 164, 165
  huampo gelatin 172, 173
huancaína 245
huarango 56–57, 245
  huarango crystals 235
  tree & sweet algae 78, 79
huarango crystals 235
  diversity of maize 68, 69
huarango molasses
  huarango crystals 235
  tree & sweet algae 78, 79
huatia 99, 245
huito 189, 245
  flying potato 228, 229
  huito dye 210, 211

I
ice cream bean see **shimbillo**
ice cream
  tree & sweet algae 78, 79
ichu
  ichu [recipe] 148, 149
  tocosh [recipe] 126, 127
infusión solar de maíz morado 76, 77

K
kañiwa / cañiwa / cañihua 245
kelp see **sargazo**
kiwicha (amaranth) 245
  alpaca & amaranth 134, 135
  avocado & seeds 84, 85

L
lapa (limpet) 245
leaves of the Andean Valley 88, 89
leche de tigre 245
lechuga de mar (sea lettuce) 246
  scallop fossil 60, 61
  tree & sweet algae 78, 79
lemon verbena see **cedrón**
lemongrass see **hierba luisa**
lengua piedra 48, 49
lettuce
  harvest & gathering 36, 37
lima beans see **pallar**
limes
  tiger's milk 30

limpets
  spiders of the rock 28, 29
linaza (flax) 246
llama y clorofila 145, 146
llama
  llama & chlorophyll 145, 146
  yellow tubers 86, 87
loche 246
lomo saltado 246
lucuma, cactus y retama 92, 93
lúcuma 246
  lúcuma, cactus & retama 92, 93

M
maca 246
  rose apple [recipe] 202, 203
macambo 246
  sapote, ungurahui & macambo 218, 219
madera y cacao 232, 233
maíz morado 246
  solar infusion of purple corn 76, 77
maize, diversity of 68, 69
malva 246
  leaves of the Andean Valley 88, 89
manayupa 246
manglar (o m / o ft) 42–44
  mangrove soil 50, 51
  rock of the mangroves 52, 53
  stone tongue 48, 49
mangrove *see* **manglar**
mangrove soil 50, 51
manioc *see* **yuca**
maracuyá (passion fruit) 246
marañon (cashew) 246
Maras salt
  extreme stems 104, 105
  fermentation in the Andes 128, 129
  heart 118, 119
  ocas and ollucos in Maras 102, 103
Marcona (–25 m / –82 ft) 26–27
  harvest & gathering 36, 37
  octopus in its coral 31, 32
  spiders of the rock 28, 29
  tiger's milk 30
markhu / markho / marko / marco 246
masas de coca 166, 167
mashua / mashwa 246
  pork in mashuas 112, 113
  sweet mashua 114, 115
  yacón root & duck 226, 227
matico 247
meat *see* **alpaca; beef; guanaco; llama**
medicinal plants
  abuta 242
  airampo 242
  ajosquiro 242
  atadijo 242
  ayahuasca 242
  ayasisa 242
  boldo 243
  borraja 243
  caigua 243
  cedrón 243
  chincho 243
  chiric sanango 244
  chuchuhuasi / chuchuwasha 244

clavo huasca 244
congona 244
culén 244
dale dale 245
hercampuri 245
hierba luisa 245
huacatay 245
huamanpinta 245
huamanripa 245
linaza 246
maca 246
malva 246
manayupa 246
markhu 246
mashua 246
matico 247
mullaca 247
muña 247
queñal 247
retama 248
ruda 248
sacha ajo 248
shimbillo 248
tocosh 124, 128, 249
uña de gato 249
miel de palo 247
miel en la jungla 222, 223
molle 247
moraya *see* **chuño**
mucílago de cacao 247
mullaca 247
muña 247
  gathering of cushuro 136, 137
  huampo gelatin 172, 173
  leaves of the Andean Valley 88, 89
  tin tin [recipe] 132, 133
mushrooms
  callampa 243
  yellow tubers 86, 87

N
nuts
  castaña 243
  marañon 246
  sacha inchi 248

O
oca 247
  extreme stems 104, 105
  ocas and ollucos in Maras 102, 103
  queñual paper 108, 109
ocas y ollucos en maras 102, 103
octopus in its coral 31, 32
olluco / ulluku / papalisa 247
  extreme stems 104, 105
  ocas and ollucos in Maras 102, 103
  ollucos & cacao 178, 179
ollucos y cacao 178, 179
orilla (85 m / 279 ft) 56–57
  cactus gel 74, 75
  cassava starch 64, 65
  diversity of maize 68, 69
  huarango crystals 235
  pacae crystals 234
  scallop fossil 60, 61
  shells in the desert 72, 73
  solar infusion of purple corn 76, 77
  tree & sweet algae 78, 79

P
paca *see* **tucunaré**
pacae 247
  pacae crystals 234
  scallop fossil 60, 61
  tree & sweet algae 78, 79
pacae crystals 234
  red Amazon 176, 177
  scallop fossil 60, 61
paiche 247
  red Amazon 176, 177
paico (epazote) 247
  gathering of cushuro 136, 137
  leaves of the Andean Valley 88, 89
  pseudocereals [recipe] 154, 155
  sweet mashua 114, 115
  tin tin [recipe] 132, 133
  yellow tubers 86, 87
pallar (lima beans / butter beans) 247
palto y las semillas 84, 85
panela 247
papa *see* **potato** 247
papa voladora 247
  flying potato 228, 229
  rose apple [recipe] 202, 203
papalisa *see* **olluco**
papeles de queñual 108, 109
pardo corn
  diversity of maize 68, 69
passion fruit *see* **maracuyá**
pata de gallo 247
  scallop fossil 60, 61
  shells in the desert 72, 73
pejerrey
  fish of high-altitude waters 158, 159
pepino melón 247
  mangrove soil 50, 51
perla corn
  diversity of maize 68, 69
Peruvian cuisine (traditional)
  aguardiente 242
  ceviche / cebiche 243
  charqui 243
  chicha de jora 243
  chuño 244
  huancaína 245
  huatia 99, 245
  lomo saltado 246
  tiradito 249
  tocosh 124, 128, 249
  tunta 140–141, 249
  uchucuta 249
pez de aguas de altitud 158, 159
pomarrosa (rose apple) 247
  rose apple [recipe] 202, 203
pork in mashuas 112, 113
potatoes 247
  chuño 244
  tocosh [recipe] 126, 127
  tunta 140–141, 249
  varieties used for *tunta* 150
prickly pear
  shells in the desert 72, 73
  stone tongue 48, 49
pseudocereales 154, 155
pseudocereals
  kañiwa 245
  kiwicha 245

pseudocereals [recipe] 154, 155
quinoa 248
pulpo en su coral 31, 32
purple corn
diversity of maize 68, 69
solar infusion of purple corn 76, 77
purslane
rock of the mangroves 52, 53

Q
quebranta 247
queñual 247
queñual paper 108, 109
quinoa 248
coca dough 166, 167
diversity of quinoas 144, 145
gathering of cushuro 136, 137
pseudocereals [recipe] 154, 155

R
raiz yacón y pato 226, 227
razor clams
mangrove soil 50, 51
recolección de cushuro 136, 137
red Amazon 176, 177
red oxalis 248
gathering of cushuro 136, 137
leaves of the Andean Valley 88, 89
queñual paper 108, 109
red Amazon 176, 177
retama 248
leaves of the Andean Valley 88, 89
lúcuma, cactus & retama 92, 93
rice, costeño 244
octopus in its coral 31, 32
roca de manglar 52, 53
rock of the mangroves 52, 53
rocoto 248
roots and tubers
arracacha 242
dale dale 245
maca 246
mashua 246
mullaca 247
oca 247
olluco 247
tocosh 124, 128, 249
yacón 249
yellow tubers 86, 87
yuca 249
rose apple see **pomarrosa**
ruda 248
bombonaje [recipe] 170, 171
red Amazon 176, 177

S
sacha ajo 248
sacha culantro / jungle culantro /
false culantro 248
sapote, ungurahui & macambo 218,
219
sacha inchi 248
sacha inchi oil
blood of the tree 196, 197
bombonaje [recipe] 170, 171
gamitana [recipe] 198, 199
gathering of cushuro 136, 137
tucunaré [recipe] 206, 207

sachapapa see **papa voladora**
sachatomate see **tomate de árbol**
salicornia (samphire / sea bean) 248
rock of the mangroves 52, 53
samphire see **salicornia**
Sandia coffee 248
sangre de árbol 196, 197
sangre de grado 248
blood of the tree 196, 197
sapote, ungurahui y macambo 218, 219
sapote 248
sapote, ungurahui & macambo 218,
219
sargazo (kelp) 248
harvest & gathering 36, 37
saúco 248
scallops
scallop fossil 60, 61
shells in the desert 72, 73
sea bean see **salicornia**
sea bubble see **cerebro de mar**
sea lettuce see **lechuga de mar**
seaweed see **algae**
sheep's milk
fish of high-altitude waters 158, 159
shells in the desert 72, 73
shimbillo (ice cream bean) 248
yacón root & duck 226, 227
shore see **orilla**
snails
churo 197, 244
solar infusion of purple corn 76, 77
soursop see **guanábana**
spiders of the rock 28, 29
squash
loche 246
stevia 248
gathering of cushuro 136, 137
huampo gelatin 172, 173
stevia crystals 238
stevia crystals 238
lúcuma, cactus & retama 92, 93
rose apple [recipe] 202, 203
stone tongue 48, 49
suelo de mangle 50, 51
sweet mashua 114, 115
sweetcorn see **corn**
sweet potatoes
spiders of the rock 28, 29
sweeteners
cacao crystals 240
chancaca 243
huarango crystals 235
pacae crystals 234
panela 247
stevia crystals 238
yacón crystals 239

T
tahuari bark (for macerations) 181
tallos extremos 104, 105
tamarillo see **tomate de árbol**
taperiba
fruits, seeds & chocolate 230, 231
tapioca flour (cassava starch) 64, 65
avocado & seeds 84, 85
cacao crystals 240
huarango crystals 235

pacae crystals 234
stevia crystals 238
wood & cacao 232, 233
yacón crystals 239
tara 249
tarwi 249
pork in mashuas 112, 113
thickeners
cactus gel 74, 75
cassava starch 64, 65
tunta thickener 150
tiger's milk 30
tin tín 249
tin tin [recipe] 132, 133
tiradito 249
tocosh 124, 128, 249
fermentation in the Andes 128, 129
tocosh [recipe] 126, 127
tomate de árbol (tamarillo) 248
avocado & seeds 84, 85
yellow tubers 86, 87
tree & sweet algae 78, 79
trees see also **bark**
abuta 242
aguaje 242
ajosquiro 242
algarrobo 242
atadijo 242
chuchuhuasi / chuchuwasha 244
huampo 172, 245
huarango 56-57, 245
pacae 247
queñal 247
shimbillo 248
tara 249
ungurahui 249
tubers see **roots and tubers**
tucunaré / paca 249
tucunaré [recipe] 206, 207
tumbo 249
diversity of maize 68, 69
scallop fossil 60, 61
tuna see **cactus**
tunta 140-141, 249
altiplano clay [recipe] 151, 152
fish of high-altitude waters 158, 159
ichu [recipe] 148, 149
quality of, categories 150
tunta thickener 150

U
uchucuta 249
uña de gato 249
ungurahui 249
sapote, ungurahui & macambo 218,
219
tucunaré [recipe] 206, 207
ungurahui dye 204, 205
wood & cacao 232, 233

W
wood & cacao 232, 233

Y
yacón 249
carachama & yacón 194, 195
yacón crystals 239
yacón root & duck 226, 227

yacón crystals 239
sweet mashua 114, 115
yacuruna caspi bark (for macerations)
181
yams
papa voladora 247
yellow tubers 86, 87
yuca (cassava / manioc) 249
cassava starch 64, 65
see also **tapioca flour**
yuyo 249
avocado & seeds 84, 85
carachama & yacón 194, 195
octopus in its coral 31, 32
pork in mashuas 112, 113
scallop fossil 60, 61
spiders of the rock 28, 29
tiger's milk 30
tree & sweet algae 78, 79

Z
zúngaro see **doncella**

RECIPE NOTES

- All herbs are fresh, unless otherwise specified.
- All cream is 36–40% fat heavy whipping cream unless otherwise specified.
- All milk is full-fat (whole) at 3% fat, homogenized and lightly pasteurized, unless otherwise specified.
- All yeast is fresh, unless otherwise specified.
- All salt is fine sea salt, unless otherwise specified.
- Bread crumbs are always dried, unless otherwise specified.

- Cooking times are for guidance only, as individual ovens vary. If using a fan (convection) oven, follow the manufacturer's instructions concerning oven temperatures.

- Exercise a high level of caution when following recipes involving any potentially hazardous activity, including the use of high temperatures, open flames, slaked lime, and when deep-frying. In particular, when deep-frying, add food carefully to avoid splashing, wear long sleeves, and never leave the pan unattended.

- Some recipes include raw or very lightly cooked eggs, meat, or fish, and fermented products. These should be avoided by the elderly, infants, pregnant women, convalescents, and anyone with an impaired immune system.

- Exercise caution when making fermented products, ensuring all equipment is spotlessly clean, and seek expert advice if in any doubt.

- When no quantity is specified, for example of oils, salts, and herbs used for finishing dishes or for deep-frying, quantities are discretionary and flexible.

- All herbs, shoots, flowers and leaves should be picked fresh from a clean source.

- Exercise caution when foraging for ingredients; any foraged ingredients should only be eaten if an expert has deemed them safe to eat.

- Both metric and imperial measures are used in this book. Follow one set of measurements throughout, not a mixture, as they are not interchangeable.

ACKNOWLEDGMENTS

Without question, to understand why and how I have done the things that I have done, there are countless people and situations that have guided me to chart a course of my own. I'm certain that all these people have helped create this book with me and the beautiful work we do together.

To the most beautiful people of this wonderful country, living off their land and food in a way that's so real, honest and authentic, they are our guides in every moment, or our examples for life. To artisans, producers, and all the guardians of this ancestral knowledge that teach us to live better every day and understand that we all live fully connected, from one person to the next. I would like to thank my chef colleagues of this hemisphere, with all of the paradoxes we experience as we continue to cook better, unite, and fight the battles that arise and will arise. It is an honor to share conversations and collaborations with you and I'm sure we will know many more.

Mater Iniciativa, the soul of everything we do at Central, surely has given us more life in these years of travels and expeditions. I thank the tremendous curiosity that has been generated as a team. Of course, Karime, for always being there, and the faithful base group of Peter, Gabriela, Paulo, and Brick, as well as all who have helped in different challenges at different times of the year.

The Central family, all of the cooks and front of the house team that I have pushed and confused so many times to run the plates, while understanding the altitudes and the complexity of these unknown products. There's Carlos, Luis, Gabriel, Juan Luis, Annia, Mariana, Joseph, Andre, and all of our amazing young team that is searching for something more than just being in a great restaurant. This book is certainly part of everyone who has literally laid the first bricks of the restaurant, managed the construction, overseen purchases, learned about expenses, and been there with me to close the restaurant every night, like Carlos Cáceres.

Malena, my dear sister who, with her sweetness, never let us reach an endpoint, but continued to inspire us to record, aim, and measure any aspect of nature that could translate into knowledge. Her sensitivity and ability to adapt to multiple disciplines with the things we encounter is outstanding, not to mention her skill of understanding my own confusions.

My wife, my best cook, Pia, who has not only endured all the difficulties and transitions since we opened Central, but has had to deal with my obsessions, my extremes, and all the times when I disappear and find myself submerged in an idea, a concept, or whatever important or inconsequential impulse. She ensures that the day-to-day details of the kitchen function in a way that I never could. Her working ability, temperament in the kitchen, and manner of respecting and inspiring every young cook, with codes and hierarchies that only she knows, has liberated me from all that occurs in the routine nature of a restaurant kitchen.

My dear Raules, our two lawyers. Blanca, Malena, and Maria Paz, three artists of everything, for everything they gave me at home. I don't think it was easy to coexist with my hyperactivity and contradictions when I was younger. They never threw in the towel and for them I am here.

Emily, Olga, and the Phaidon team, from start to finish, you tried to put everything in order and all flowed calmly. The confidence in us and the freedom you allowed have been a key to this project.

To Nicholas Gill, a great friend, the one who made it so we could communicate and enjoy this work of Central and Mater Initiative. Our work together involved altitude sickness, periods of isolation, confusion by remoteness, a lack of sleep, and other abnormal situations that became enriching. Work of this intensity always generates special friendships. Thanks, Nick.

To my son, Cristobal, who I can only say that when I begin to think a lot about work that can change the world, there is a little person that is working to change me.

Phaidon Press Limited
Regent's Wharf
All Saints Street
London N1 9PA

Phaidon Press Inc.
65 Bleecker Street
New York, NY 10012

phaidon.com

First published 2016
© 2016 Phaidon Press Limited

ISBN 978 0 7148 7280 3

A CIP catalogue record for this book is
available from the British Library and the
Library of Congress.

Commissioning Editor: Emily Takoudes
Project Editor: Olga Massov
Production Controller: Leonie Kellman
Photography: Jimena Agois (food),
Ernesto Benavides (landscape)

Phaidon would like to thank Evelyn
Battaglia and Kate Slate for their
contributions to this book.

Design: Atlas

Printed in China

Virgilio Martínez opened Central,
in Lima, in 2009. He was named the
number one chef in Latin America
and number four around the world by
the World's 50 Best. He is the founder
of Mater Iniciativa, which researches
and catalogues indigenous foods
in Peru. He also runs the restaurants
Lima and Lima Floral in London.
He lives in Peru.

MARCONA

MANGLAR

ORILLA

BAJO ANDINO

ANDE